CASEBOOKS PUBLISHED

Austen: *Emma*   DAVID LODGE
Austen: *'Northanger Abbey' & 'Persuasion'*   B.C. SOUTHAM
Austen: *'Sense and Sensibility', 'Pride and Prejudice' & 'Mansfield Park'*   B.C. SOUTHAM
Blake: *Songs of Innocence and Experience*   MARGARET BOTTRALL
Charlotte Brontë: *'Jane Eyre' & 'Villette'*   MIRIAM ALLOTT
Emily Brontë *Wuthering Heights*   MIRIAM ALLOTT
Browning: *'Men and Women' & Other Poems*   J.R. WATSON
Bunyan: *Pilgrim's Progress*   ROGER SHARROCK
Chaucer   *Canterbury Tales*   J.J. ANDERSON
Coleridge

Congre
Conrac
Conrac
Dicken
Dicken
Donne
George
George
T.S. El
T.S. El
T.S. El
Farquh
Fieldin
Forster
Hardy:
Hardy:
Hopkir
James:
Jonson
Jonson
Joyce:
Keats:
Keats:
D.H. L
D.H. L
Marlov
Marlov
   BROV
Marvel
Milton:
Milton:
Osborn
Peacocl
Pope: 7
Shakes
Shakes
Shakes
Shakes
Shakes
Shakespeare: *Henry V*   MICHAEL QUINN
Shakespeare: *Julius Caesar*   PETER URE

Comedy
Developments in Criticism

A CASEBOOK

EDITED BY

D. J. PALMER

MACMILLAN

First published 1984 by
Higher and Further Education Division
MACMILLAN PUBLISHERS LTD
London and Basingstoke
Companies and representatives throughout the world

Typeset by
Wessex Typesetters Ltd
Frome, Somerset

Printed in Hong Kong

British Library Cataloguing in Publication Data
Comedy.—(Casebook series)
  1. English literature—History and criticism
  2. Comedy
  I. Palmer, D.J.   II. Series
  820'.9'17   PR469.C/
  ISBN 0–333–26901–2
  ISBN 0–333–26902–0 Pbk

CONTENTS

Continued

Part Three: *Twentieth-Century Views*

GENERAL EDITOR'S PREFACE

The Casebook series, launched in 1968, has become a well-regarded library of critical studies. The central concern of the series remains the 'single-author' volume, but suggestions from the academic community have led to an extension of the original plan, to include occasional volumes on such general themes as literary 'schools' and genres.

Each volume in the central category deals either with one well-known and influential work by an individual author, or with closely related works by one writer. The main section consists of critical readings, mostly modern, collected from books and journals. A selection of reviews and comments by the author's contemporaries is also included, and sometimes comment from the author himself. The Editor's Introduction charts the reputation of the work or works from the first appearance to the present time.

Volumes in the 'general themes' category are variable in structure but follow the basic purpose of the series in presenting an integrated selection of readings, with an Introduction which explores the themes and discusses the literary and critical issues involved.

A single volume can represent no more than a small selection of critical opinions. Some critics are excluded for reasons of space, and it is hoped that readers will pursue the suggestions for further reading in the Select Bibliography. Other contributions are severed from their original context, to which some readers may wish to turn. Indeed, if they take a hint from the critics represented here, they certainly will.

A. E. DYSON

INTRODUCTION

The excerpts selected for this Casebook illuminate the traditions of comic theory in European and, more particularly, in English literature. Although comedy in its strictest sense is a dramatic genre, some discussion of its counterpart in the novel is included, together with modern studies of its non-literary antecedents and analogues, where these are relevant to an understanding of comedy in general. The emphasis of the anthology is on the historical development of the theory of comedy. Little space has therefore been given to psychological investigations of laughter, and none at all to the art of comic performance. Many of the excerpts are from longer works which it is hoped the reader will wish to consult.

*

On the face of it, one of the strangest notions about comedy must surely be Ben Jonson's assertion that, according to Aristotle, 'the moving of laughter is a fault in Comedie'.* Aristotle, of course, said no such thing, and everyone knows that it is the business of comedy to make us laugh, and everyone enjoys a good laugh. The trouble is that laughter can be remarkably offensive and can end in tears. As Elder Olson points out, 'a great many jokes are really kinds of aggression; those who laugh at them laugh because they feel hatred for the object ridiculed, and hatred is always of something painful; and other people are offended by jokes of this order'. Comic laughter therefore runs certain risks, and some of the greatest comedy is perilously close to tears, of bitterness, of anger, of despair. The theory of comedy, therefore, as exemplified in the following pages, is largely concerned with making out the case for safe laughter, with justifying the proper grounds for comedy. Jonson's misgivings might be overstated, but they are not altogether misplaced.

* The absence of a source reference for a quotation in this Introduction signifies that it is taken from an item in the Casebook. The references for other quotations are listed in the Notes at the end of the Introduction.

The history of comic theory could be regarded as a series of variations on the basic conception that comedy involves a sense of triumph over whatever is inimical to human or social good, however this ideal is defined. The modifications and metamorphoses of this conception are innumerable, but by and large there are two major categories of comic theory. The first of these to establish itself in critical tradition is the notion of laughter as the ridicule of some deficiency or error which can be shown as foolish. Scornful laughter of this kind is obviously aggressive and therefore its painfulness is usually mitigated in theory by an appeal to its instructive or corrective function. The other main theoretical category relates comedy to festive rejoicing, in which laughter is convivial and fooling is in order. Here the potentially anarchic and subversive spirit of carnival is licensed as a celebration of the life-force triumphing over its enemies.

The brief remarks of Plato and Aristotle hardly amount to a fully-fledged critique of comedy, but they are seminal insights, initiating the theory of laughter as ridicule. Plato's discussion of 'the state of mind in which we listen to a comedy' occurs, significantly, in a section of the *Philebus* concerned with the mixed sensations of pleasure and pain. In singling out the lack of self-knowledge as the target of ridicule, Plato relates laughter to critical intelligence, but he is careful to confine the ridiculous to weak characters incapable of taking vengeance on the scoffer. Otherwise, in the strong the same fault is not ridiculous but 'odious and repulsive'. Plato is clearly aware of the aggressive element in 'playful malice'. Aristotle – whose pithy but elliptical remarks on comedy in the *Poetics*[1] are incidental to his monumental analysis of tragedy – generalises the notion of 'the Ludicrous' as 'a defect or ugliness', implying a departure from the norm, a kind of inferiority to ourselves. He also follows Plato in excluding whatever is 'painful or destructive'. Cicero similarly rules out both 'outstanding wickedness' and 'outstanding wretchedness' as unsuitable subjects for ridicule.

From these sparse beginnings, the classical tradition of comic theory, based on the concept of the ludicrous, was to be revived and developed in the Renaissance. Meanwhile, however, other ideas of comedy were formulated which had little to do with the business of laughter. The grammarians of late antiquity are hardly remembered today in the history of criticism, but one of their works, a treatise entitled 'De Tragœdia et Comœdia', is of considerable importance in the transmission of critical doctrine since it was frequently included in the early printed editions of the comedies of Terence.[2] The treatise, which dates from the fourth century AD, is in fact a compilation of two separate essays, one by a certain Evanthius and the other by Donatus, to whom it was solely attributed since he was also the author of the Life of Terence and of the textual commentary that were included in editions of the plays. The grammarians were not original critical theorists but scholars incorporating in their work a received body of knowledge. Quotation from accepted authority and demonstration by etymology are characteristic of their methods. Thus, in the short extract by which the treatise is represented here, the definition of comedy attributed to 'the Greeks' actually comes from another grammarian, Diomedes, while that attributed to Cicero cannot be traced to any of his known works, although it became widely disseminated in the Renaissance. So also did the view that comedy deals with the everyday life of ordinary people, while tragedy is something that happens to the nobility in their 'kingly halls'. This socio-logical distinction between the two genres seems partly a mis-understanding of Aristotle's reference to characters 'of a lower type' and partly an inference drawn from the etymological association of comedy with *kōmē*, meaning a village. Aristotle himself first proposed this possible derivation, together with the alternative, from *kōmōs*, meaning a festive procession. Most modern scholars would argue for the latter, as the excerpt from F.M. Cornford's study of the origins of Greek comedy suggests.

The most significant contribution of the grammarians to comic theory is the idea that comedy is instructive. According to Evanthius, it teaches 'what is of use in life, on the one hand, and what must be avoided, on the other'. This is said without any reference to the use of ridicule, but it is clearly an important link between the insights of Plato and Aristotle and the sub-sequent neo-classical view of comedy as corrective laughter. After all, if comedy gives us useful lessons, its aggressiveness is that much more acceptable. As Eric Bentley observes, 'it is might backed by the conviction of right'.

In the centuries which intervened between the grammarians and the resurgence of classical theory, the conception of comedy became divorced both from the drama and from the ludicrous. Dante's *Epistle to Can Grande* is quite representative of the medieval view in its definition of comedy as 'a certain genre of poetic narrative' which 'introduces a situation of adversity, but ends in prosperity'. The influence of the grammarians in the development of this view is evident in the schematic categorising of antitheses between comedy and tragedy. Nevertheless, while it might seem difficult to find any connection between the medieval definition and the classical idea of the ludicrous, Dante's way of thinking about comedy is far from being an eccentric detour in the history of criticism. In relation to his own *Divine Comedy*, for instance, it is closely analogous to those early dramatic rituals in which F.M. Cornford finds the origins of comedy, celebrating 'the victory of the Spirit of life over the adverse influences of blight and death'. More surprisingly perhaps, it is also echoed in the words of Eric Bentley: 'The comic dramatist's starting point is misery; the joy at his destination is a superb and thrilling transcendence.'

Another medieval concept survives in the Prologue to Nicholas Udall's *Ralph Roister Doister*, ironically enough since his play, usually regarded as the first English comedy, was written in imitation of Terence:

> For Mirth prolongeth life, and causeth health,
> Mirth recreates our spirits and voideth pensiveness,
> Mirth increaseth amity, not hindering our wealth.

'Mirth' is not scornful laughter but the merriment of pastime and game. So, for instance, Chaucer's Host in *The Canterbury Tales* uses the word when he proposes that the pilgrims tell each other tales on their way to Canterbury:

> Fayn wolde I doon yow myrthe, wiste I how,
> And of myrthe I am right now bythoght,
> To doon yow ese, and it shal coste noght. [3]

Shakespeare also refers to the curative properties of 'mirth' in

the Induction to *The Taming of the Shrew*, when the players
arrive to entertain Christopher Sly:

> Your honour's players, hearing your amendment,
> Are come to play a pleasant comedy;
> For so your doctors hold it very meet,
> Seeing too much sadness hath congeal'd your blood,
> And melancholy is the nurse of frenzy.
> Therefore they thought it good you hear a play
> And frame your mind to mirth and merriment,
> Which bars a thousand harms and lengthens life. ⁴

There are no aggressive connotations in such a notion of comedy
(although there is plenty of aggression in *The Taming of the Shrew*
itself), which belongs to the popular native tradition and
evidently reflects comedy's associations with festive revelry.
Even a century and a half later, Henry Fielding departs from
neo-classical concern with the ludicrous proper to defend burlesque on the grounds that 'it contributes more to exquisite
mirth and laughter than any other; and these are probably
more wholesome physic for the mind, and conduce better to
purge away spleen, melancholy, and ill affections, than is
generally imagined'.

The learned tradition of comic theory was, however, that of
neo-classicism. Sidney's definition of comedy in *An Apology for
Poetry* succinctly expresses the orthodox view:

Comedy is an imitation of the common errors of our life, which he
representeth in the most ridiculous and scornefull sort that may be; so as it is
impossible that any beholder can be content to be such a one. ⁵

It is 'bitter and profitable', in Ben Jonson's phrase. Yet Sidney's
distinction between 'laughter' and 'delight' and Jonson's distinction between buffoonery and 'jests that are true and naturall' depend on that principle of comic decorum which led Aristotle to exclude from the ludicrous whatever is 'painful and
destructive'. Jonson alludes to what had become the standard
contrast between the coarseness and scurrility of the so-called
Old Comedy (associated with Aristophanes) and the greater
civility and refinement of the so-called New Comedy (associated
with Menander and his Roman imitators, Terence and Plautus). Another Renaissance critic, George Puttenham, gives a

useful summary of this conventional comparison between out-
landish laughter and its more acceptable counterpart:

And this kind of poeme was called Comedy, and followed next after the
Satyre, openly and by expresse names taxing men more maliciously and
impudently then became, so as they were enforced for feare of quarrell and
blame to disguise their players with strange apparell, and by colouring their
faces and carying hatts and capps of diverse fashions to make themselves lesse
knowen. But as time and experience do reform every thing that is amisse, so
this bitter poeme called the Old Comedy, being disused and taken away, the
new Comedy came in place, more civil and pleasant a great deale, and not
touching any man by name, but in a certaine generalitie glancing at every
abuse, so as from thenceforth fearing none illwill or enmitie at any bodies
hands, they left aside their disguisings and played bare face.   [6]

Because scornful laughter is basically aggressive, the theory of
the ludicrous generates what Elder Olson calls 'classification of
humor as gross or refined, brutal or humane, intelligent or
stupid or silly, or the like'. The balance between pain and
pleasure is a delicate issue for this tradition of comic theory. As
Olson says, 'standards vary, for they are opinions of what is
right and proper in any given instance, and such opinions vary
with the class and education, intelligence and character and so
on, of the people who hold them'. They can also vary from one
generation to the next. For all these reasons, by the time Congreve was writing, there were many who found Restoration
Comedy gross rather than refined, more offensive than pleasing,
and the prolonged reaction against scornful laughter, on the
stage at least, had already commenced.

Congreve, like earlier Restoration dramatists, claims to be
writing in the English or Jonsonian tradition of the 'humours',
'which naturally arise, from the different Constitutions, Com-
plexions and Dispositions of Men'. Neo-classicism encouraged
the theory of imitating Nature, though in fact dramatic convention was at least as important in providing the character-types
who appear and again in the comedies of the period. Fielding's
acknowledgement that 'we should ever confine ourselves to
nature' in true comedy, and Goldsmith's reference to 'that
natural portrait of Human Folly and Frailty, of which all are
judges, because all have sat for the picture', reflect a similar
disregard for the formal considerations that determine comic

characterisation and make our responses to the stage-represen-
tation of, say, young love and parental opposition or prodigality
and frugality very different from our responses to such matters
in real life. At the same time, these later spokesmen for classical
comic theory have, as it were, a lower pain-threshold than their
Renaissance predecessors. They say little about the instructive
or corrective function of laughter. To Congreve, the painful is
whatever offends a refined sense of our common humanity: 'I
can never care for seeing things that force me to entertain low
thoughts of my Nature. I dont know how it is with others, but
I confess freely to you, I could never look long upon a Monkey,
without very Mortifying Reflections.' The desire to take a more
benign view of the ridiculous is also evident in Fielding's defence
of burlesque since it confers 'good-humour and benevolence'
upon its audience, while his narrow identification of 'the true
source of the ridiculous' with affectation probably arises from
his intention to expose in *Joseph Andrews* what he considered to be
the false morality of Samuel Richardson's puritanism in *Pamela,
Or Virtue Rewarded* (1740). Puritanism and sentimentalism are
the natural enemies of comedy.

The attenuation of the neo-classical idea of the ludicrous,
which is evident from the time of Congreve onwards, and the
growing distaste for scornful or aggressive laughter, underlie the
attitudes adopted by Hazlitt, Lamb and, later in the nineteenth
century, Meredith. Hazlett's ironic pretence that comedy, 'by
constantly and successfully exposing the follies and weakness of
mankind to ridicule, in the end leaves itself nothing worth
laughing at' implies that the old notion of corrective laughter
can no longer be taken seriously. 'The proper subject of ridicule
is *egotism*', he writes, while wishing nostalgically that egotism
was still around to be laughed at, instead of the 'tame, correct
and spiritless' manners of his own age. Hazlitt's kind of laughter
is affectionate and sympathetic, cherishing rather than chasten-
ing the foibles of flamboyant individualism. Lamb's removal of
Restoration Comedy from the sphere of moral concerns counter-
acts a tendency (which still exists) to take it too seriously, but it
also diminishes 'those sports of a witty fancy' to elegant and
innocuous trifles. In the suggestion that their sophisticated *in-
souciance* redeems the plays and their characters from un-

pleasantness might be heard an echo of the traditional opposition between grossness and refinement in comedy.

Meredith's sense of 'the most subtle delicacy' required of the comic poet is also refined to the point of fastidiousness: 'The laughter of satire is a blow in the back or the face. The laughter of Comedy is impersonal and of unrivalled politeness.' Such laughter appeals to the intelligence rather than to the aggressive instincts. According to Meredith, comedy is civilised and civilising not so much because it exposes folly to ridicule (although he does mention some of the traditional corrective functions of comic laughter) as because it presents men and women in the equilibrium of contention for their social rights. Meredith's admiration for the self-reliant heroines of comedy ('not necessarily heartless from being clear-sighted') and his emphasis upon the sophisticated nature of comic laughter reflect his rather narrow identification of his rarefied 'Comic spirit' with the comedy of wit, particularly that of the Restoration period. As Ian Donaldson points out, however, such an assumption of a direct *rapport* between art and life can be highly misleading, since comedy often presents an inverted image of social realities.

With Henri Bergson we come to the beginning of modern comic theory, although there is much in keeping with traditional ideas of the corrective and civilising functions of comedy in his description of laughter as 'a sort of *social gesture*' which 'pursues a utilitarian aim of general improvement'. His identification of 'rigidity', 'the easy automatism of acquired habits', as the source of the ludicrous is useful when applied to the comedy of obsessive, eccentric or stereotyped behaviour. But for that very reason, as Eric Bentley suggests, there are limits to its appropriateness: 'When one puts down the book one realises that this dazzling piece of theory leaves no room in comic writing for Shakespeare.' Not all comedy sets out to ridicule, and there is sympathetic as well as scornful laughter. Nevertheless, Bergson is modern in offering an interpretation of the ludicrous. Where earlier writers assume it as a self-evident property inherent in certain kinds of behaviour, Bergson speculates on the motivation of laughter. Moreover, his attribution of that motive to society's insistence 'on a constant striving after reciprocal adaptation', while it is a peculiarly abstract principle, liberates comic theory from its long enslavement to morality and anticipates the amoral vitalism of twentieth-century approaches to the subject.

Despite the diversity of twentieth-century contributions to comic theory, some shared concerns and emphases emerge. In particular, there has been a growing interest in the formal conventions and traditions of the genre. Modern discussions of comedy, distanced as they are from the neo-classical preoccupations with comic decorum and the ridicule of folly, have revived the question of its origins and its relations with other literary and non-literary forms. They have explored its basic structural patterns and mechanisms, greatly extending our awareness that there is much more to comedy than the raising of laughter. Moreover, for some of these writers, the advent of black comedy and the theatre of the absurd has raised afresh the ambivalent nature of comic laughter. To clarify some of the main lines of development, the twentieth-century contributors represented here have been divided into two groups. The first of these sub-divisions, headed 'Traditions of Comedy', includes those contributors who are chiefly interested in historical aspects of comedy, its prototypes and analogues. The other sub-division, 'Conceptions of Comic Form', is mainly concerned with theoretical positions and problems, some more systematically defined than others. Of course this division is not watertight and, like the chronological sequence in which the excerpts are ordered, it will occasionally need to be overridden by cross-reference.

The importance of ancient myth and ritual for an understanding of the evolution of Greek and therefore European drama was a rediscovery of late nineteenth-century scholarship. New lines of investigation were stimulated by the cross-fertilisation of traditional classical studies with younger branches of learning such as comparative religion and anthropology. F. M. Cornford's book, *The Origin of Attic Comedy*, is a product of this phase of scholarship, referring not only to connections between the comedies of Aristophanes and earlier Greek fertility rites, but also to parallels with ceremonial customs in other cultures, including those still to be found among the Swedes and the Eskimos. The significance of Cornford's approach, as a contribution to the theory of comedy, lies not in the precise detail of his historical reconstruction but in his general perception of an association between comedy and the theme of the triumphant renewal of life, celebrated in various types of archaic games and rituals. For this approach dislodges the notion of the ludicrous from the central place it had occupied in comic theory (with the exceptions already noted) since Aristotle, although Aristotle himself had mentioned the possible etymological connection between comedy and folk-revels. Of course it is easy to recognise the close relationship and yet the distinction between the triumphant merry-making of the victorious life-force and the scornful mockery directed at the defeated enemy. Susanne Langer argues from a different stand point that comic laughter is 'a sudden heightening of the vital rhythm'.

It is not a far step from Cornford's account of 'the chief varieties of dramatic ritual associated with the renewal of life in spring' to Northrop Frye's syncretic treatment of 'the ritual pattern' of death and revival in different forms of comedy. Frye's well-known essay has had a seminal influence on the modern interpretation of comedy, Shakespearian comedy in particular. He brilliantly relates the typical plot of New Comedy, concluding with 'the birth of a renewed sense of social integration', to Shakespeare's romantic 'drama of the green world', whose theme 'is once again the triumph of life over the waste land, the death and revival of the year impersonated by figures still human, and once divine as well'. At last Shakespeare's comedies could be discussed, not as merely amusing and charming yet implausible stories, but in terms of their deeper meanings, their profounder patterns and rhythms. Even so, illuminating as its insights are, Frye's interpretative approach is not without its dangers. If comedy has not quite parted company with its remote antecedents in myth and ritual, it has certainly come a long way since, in more directions and usually with less solemnity than attends Frye's claim that 'the ritual pattern behind the catharsis of comedy is the resurrection that follows the death, the epiphany or manifestation of the risen hero'.

Frye's reference to Falstaff as 'a mock king, a lord of misrule, and his tavern [as] a Saturnalia' suggests the associations of comedy with the potentially anarchic and subversive spirit of festive fooling, aspects of which are also explored here by Walter Kaiser, Mikhail Bakhtin and Ian Donaldson. The excerpts from these three writers are complementary in their treatment of comic irreverence and irresponsibility. Kaiser describes the traditional licence of the fool, as it derives from his supposed ignorance and stupidity: 'Because the fool is not expected to *know* anything, he readily became an expression of all the mischievous and rebellious desires in man which society attempts to control or frustrate.' But Kaiser goes on to trace the ways in which Renaissance humanism and scepticism developed the paradoxical notion of wise folly, in which the self-professed fool 'manages ... to present truth by means of comedy, claiming to be wise when he laughs and to teach us wisdom when he causes laughter in us'. A similar freedom from restraint and an anti-authoritarian attitude is found by Bakhtin in the popular customs of carnival merry-making: 'carnival celebrated temporary liberation from the prevailing truth and from the established order; it marked the suspension of all hierarchical ranks, privileges, norms and prohibitions.' What Bakhtin calls the 'world-inside-out' in carnival corresponds very closely to the inverted relationships and topsy-turvy society of seventeenth-century comedy, discussed by Donaldson.

Although they are focused on particular historical periods, and only Donaldson is dealing specifically with stage-comedy, these three illustrations of comic unruliness have significance for comedy in general. Northrop Frye speaks of comedy ending in a sense of liberation from moral bondage, but it is not only in the happy resolution that there is a setting-free. As in the analogues of the fool's licence and the uninhibited revelry of carnival, comedy involves the release and the indulgence of irrepressible energies, usually sexual (Jack must have Jill if there is to be a happy ending), though often including other natural appetites. Hence the characteristic conflicts in comedy between the would-be repressive figures of authority and the hero and heroine. In comedy our sympathies lie with youth against age, with the prodigal against the miser, with the drunkard against the abstainer, with the rogue against the policemen, and so on. This sense of release is also generated by the mounting confu-

sions and cross-purposes characteristic of the comic plot, especially in the hectic pace of farce. The all-embracing conviviality
of carnival laughter, as Bakhtin describes it, is clearly related to
the way in which the comic plot presses towards social renewal
and reintegration, while the ambivalent playfulness of the fool,
in the tradition defined by Kaiser, has its counterpart in comedy's apparent refusal to take things seriously.

Looked at another way, comedy's light-heartedness and sense
of liberation imply some means of removing or at least dimin-
ishing causes for serious concern, and it is to this aspect of the
subject that R.S. Crane and Elder Olson direct our attention.
Both are neo-Aristotelian in their approach, recalling, for instance, Aristotle's exclusion from the ludicrous of whatever is
'painful or destructive'. Crane's analysis of *Tom Jones* is a mas-
terly piece of practical criticism, but it is also a demonstration
which draws conclusions of general significance for comedy.
While our sympathies lie with Tom and Sophia, Fielding allays
our anxieties for them by making their enemies ineffectual and
ridiculous, and Tom is exculpated from our censure since 'we
realise that his blunders arise from no permanent weakness of
character but are merely the natural errors of judgement, easily
corrigible in the future, of an inexperienced and too impulsively
generous and gallant young man'. This is in keeping with what
has been said above about comedy's tendency to side with
youthful exuberance against what is represented as mean-
spiritedness.

Olson's formal position is similar when he argues that the
nature of the comic involves a 'minimisation of the claim of
some particular thing to be taken seriously'. Theoretically,
therefore, nothing is inherently either comic or serious: 'It is not
the events by themselves which are matter for gravity or levity;
it is the view taken of them. ... The Oedipus legend served
Sophocles as a tragic subject; it would be quite as possible to
make it into comedy.' That is precisely what happens in New
Comedy, as Northrop Frye points out. In practice, Olson allows,
conventions and standards of judgement determine what is to
be treated light-heartedly, but whatever its subject, comedy
'removes concern by showing that it was absurd to think that
there was ground for it'.

Olson's rigorously formalist approach, which regards comedy purely as a set of special conditions that may be imposed on any subject, strongly contrasts with Susanne Langer's interpretation of the functions of comedy. Between them, in effect, Olson and Susanne Langer represent the twin polarities of comic theory. For Olson, as for Aristotle and the classical tradition, 'the comic includes only the ridiculous'. For Susanne Langer, on the other hand, 'humour ... is not the essence of comedy, but only one of its most useful and natural elements'. Laughter, when it occurs, is an intensification of our perception of 'the motion and rhythm of living'. 'The feeling of comedy is a feeling of heightened vitality', she observes, developing an argument aligned with that tradition in which the comic is associated with the embracing of life rather than with the ludicrous. Her own contribution to this conception of comedy is focussed on the problematical distinction between laughter in the theatre and laughter in other circumstances: a distinction too often overlooked. For, as Susanne Langer reminds us, laughter in comedy is not isolated and incidental but integral to the structure of the play as a whole, its 'rhythm of feeling', which is that of a specially constructed world: 'the "livingness" of the human world is abstracted, composed, and presented to us; with it the high points of the composition that are illuminated by humor'.

Finally, lest our sense of comedy is too genial and genteel, Friedrich Dürrenmatt and Eric Bentley administer a pungent antidote of modernist polemic, giving a new twist to some old ideas. If Aristotle, for instance, laid down the principle that comedy should avoid whatever is painful and destructive, then perhaps that is because comedy is a reaction to pain and destruction which registers their reality in order to surmount them. 'The world (hence the stage which represents this world) is for me something monstrous', writes Dürrenmatt, 'a riddle of misfortune which must be accepted but before which one must not capitulate.' The ancient rituals described by Cornford, celebrating 'the victory of the Spirit of life over the adverse influences of blight and death', are transformed into something less triumphant, 'an individual's decision to endure this world in which we live like Gulliver among the giants'. For this practising dramatist, 'comedy alone is suitable', not because it is a way of looking on the brighter side of life, but because its absurd inventions give form to the absurdity and formlessness of the modern world. And if comedy, according to one old-fashioned notion, is supposed to instruct through laughter, then its 'conceit' or invention 'easily transforms the crowd of theatre-goers into a mass which can be attacked, deceived, outsmarted into listening to things it would otherwise not so readily listen to'. Significantly, the fellow-dramatist invoked by Dürrenmatt is Aristophanes, but Ben Jonson might well have approved of the aggressive stance adopted here.

Eric Bentley's witty and iconoclastic essay also challenges bland assumptions about the benevolence of comedy. He begins by distinguishing between the lack of feeling in farce and 'the bitterness and sadness that so readily come to the surface in comedy'. The comic artist has to have 'an eagerness and zest in sheer being' but also 'a keen and painful awareness of the obstacles in the path'. Then, comparing comedy with tragedy, Bentley contrasts the tragic confrontation of misery and suffering with comedy's attempt to evade such unpleasant realities: 'Comedy is indirect, ironical. It says fun when it means misery. And when it lets the misery show, it is able to transcend it in joy.' Unlike the tragic poet, 'the comic poet is less apt to write out of a particular crisis than from that steady ache of misery which in human life is even more common than crisis and so a more insistent problem'. The essay is eminently quotable, and if it seems perverse and paradoxical, Bentley might argue that comedy itself is like that, preferring to express its acutest insights obliquely, playfully, pleasurably. An introduction to an anthology of comic theory ought to allow him the last word on the dangers of theorising about comedy:

I hope the foregoing generalizations are clear, but, if they are, they must also be too simple, too definite, and too schematic to correspond to all the facts. Categories, as Bernard Berenson put it, are only a compromise with chaos. And having used them, we do well to renew contact with the chaos and ask what damage a particular compromise has done.

NOTES

1. On the possibility that a second part of the *Poetics*, now lost, contained a fuller discussion of comedy, see G. M. A. Grube, *The Greek and Roman Critics* (London, 1965), p. 70; and Sir David Ross, *Aristotle* (London, 1923; paperback edn, 1964), p. 290. See also ref. in Select Bibliography to Lane Cooper, *An Aristotelian Theory of Comedy*.

2. See the account in Madeleine Doran, *Endeavors of Art: A Study of Form in Elizabethan Drama* (Madison, Wisc., 1954; paperback edn, 1964), pp. 106-8, 116.

3. General Prologue, lines 766-8: *The Complete Works of Geoffrey Chaucer*, ed. F. N. Robinson (London, n.d.).

4. Induction, scene ii, lines 126-33: *William Shakespeare: The Complete Works*, ed. P. Alexander (London, 1951).

5. Sir Philip Sidney, *An Apology for Poetry*, ed. G. Shepherd (London, 1965), p. 117.

6. George Puttenham, *The Arte of English Poesie*, ed. G. D. Willcock and A. Walker (Cambridge, 1936), pp. 31-2.

PART ONE

The Classical and Medieval Tradition

Plato (c. 350 BC)

Self-Ignorance and the Comical Spirit

SOCRATES: Or take again the state of soul in which we listen to a comedy. Has it struck you that there too is a blending of pain with pleasure?

PROTARCHUS: I fear I do not quite follow you.

SOCRATES: Why now, Protarchus; it is not so easy to remark the regular occurrences of the experience in this case.

PROTARCHUS: No, I fancy not.

SOCRATES: Still, the more obscure the point, the more carefully we should note it, if we are to become quicker to detect the blending of pain with pleasure in general.

PROTARCHUS: Well, say on.

SOCRATES: This word *malice*, which we have just used, what would you say it stands for? A kind of mental pain, or what?

PROTARCHUS: A mental pain, certainly.

SOCRATES: And yet, as you will find, the man who feels it is pleased by his neighbour's misfortune.

PROTARCHUS: Emphatically so.

SOCRATES: And ignorance and silliness, as we call it, is a misfortune.

PROTARCHUS: Of course.

SOCRATES: Now this will show you the real character of the comical.

PROTARCHUS: Pray proceed.

SOCRATES: Why, it is, to put it broadly, a vice which gets its name from a certain habit of mind, and is that particular form of this vice which exhibits the contrary of the state of soul spoken of in the inscription at Delphi.

PROTARCHUS: You mean, the motto 'Know thyself', Socrates?

SOCRATES: I do. Obviously, the inscription must intend by the contrary of that state entire ignorance of self.

PROTARCHUS: No doubt.

SOCRATES: Now, Protarchus, you must try to divide this fault into three varieties.

PROTARCHUS: By how is this to be done? I fear the task is beyond me.

SOCRATES: And so you say I must now make the division?

PROTARCHUS: Say it? Ay, and what is more, I entreat you to do so.

SOCRATES: Well, when a man is ignorant of himself, the affliction must always take one of three forms.

PROTARCHUS: And what are they?

SOCRATES: In the first place, it may be ignorance of his own finances; he may fancy his means more affluent than they are.

PROTARCHUS: A malady, I confess, from which many suffer.

SOCRATES: But even more numerous are those who imagine themselves taller and handsomer than they really are, and endowed with all kinds of unreal personal advantages.

PROTARCHUS: Very true.

SOCRATES: But the commonest form of the error, by far, I conceive, is the third, which concerns qualities of soul; a man fancies himself better in the point of virtue than he really is.

PROTARCHUS: Emphatically so.

SOCRATES: And among the virtues is not wisdom that to which the mass of mankind advances an obstinate claim which involves them in disputation and the illusory conceit of knowledge?

PROTARCHUS: Surely.

SOCRATES: Now a man would be right in calling this state of soul, in all its forms, a bad thing.

PROTARCHUS: Entirely right.

SOCRATES: Well, we have still to distinguish between two forms of it, Protarchus, if we are to observe the singular blending of pleasure with pain involved in playful malice. You ask how the distinction is to be made? It can only be with all who have this foolish false conceit of themselves, as with all the rest of mankind; some of them are endowed with strength and capacity, with others it is otherwise.

PROTARCHUS: Undeniably.

SOCRATES: Then you may make this a basis for division. Those of them who combine their delusion with weakness and incapacity to be revenged on a scoffer you may truly call *comic* figures; as for those with the strength and capacity for vengeance, you will reckon them up correctly if you describe them as dangerous and odious. In the strong, ignorance of self is odious and repulsive – it and its counterfeit presentiments are injurious to a man's neighbour as well as to himself; – where it is weak, we see the proper place and true character of the comic.

SOURCE: extract from *Philebus*, translated by A.E. Taylor (London, 1956), pp. 167–9.

Aristotle　　　(c. 335–22 BC)

On the Ludicrous

... Comedy is, as we have said, an imitation of characters of a lower type, – not, however, in the full sense of the word bad; for the Ludicrous is merely a subdivision of the ugly. It may be defined as a defect or ugliness which is not painful or destructive. Thus, for example, the comic mask is ugly and distorted, but does not cause pain. ...

SOURCE: extract from *The Poetics of Aristotle*, translated by S.H. Butcher (London, 1895), p. 19.

Cicero   (55 BC)

The Orator's Use of Laughter

... As regards laughter, there are five matters for consideration: first, its nature; second, its source; third, whether willingness to produce it becomes an orator; fourth, the limits of his licence; fifth, the classification of things laughable.

Now the first of these topics, the essential nature of laughter – the way it is occasioned, where it is seated, and how it comes into being, and bursts out so unexpectedly that, strive as we may, we cannot restrain it, and how at the same instant it takes possession of the lungs, voice, pulse, countenance and eyes – all this I leave to Democritus,[1] for it does not concern the present conversation, and, even if it did, I should still not be ashamed to show ignorance of something which even its professed expositors do not understand.

Then the field or province, so to speak, of the laughable (this being our next problem) is restricted to that which may be described as unseemly or ugly; for the chief, if not the only, objects of laughter are those sayings which remark upon and point out something unseemly in no unseemly manner.

And again, to come to our third topic, it clearly becomes an orator to raise laughter, and this on various grounds; for instance, merriment naturally wins goodwill for its author; and everyone admires acuteness, which is often concentrated in a single word, uttered generally in repelling, though sometimes in delivering, an attack; and it shatters or obstructs or makes light of an opponent, or alarms or repulses him; and it shows the orator himself to be a man of finish, accomplishment and taste; and, best of all, it relieves dullness and tones down austerity, and, by a jest or a laugh, often dispels distasteful suggestions not easily weakened by reasonings.

But the limits within which things laughable are to be handled by the orator, that fourth question we put to ourselves, is one calling for most careful consideration. For neither outstanding wickedness, such as involves crime, nor, on the other hand, outstanding wretchedness is assailed by ridicule, for the public would have the villainous hurt by a weapon rather more formidable than ridicule; while they dislike mockery of the wretched, except perhaps if these bear themselves arrogantly. And you must be especially tender of popular esteem, so that you do not inconsiderately speak ill of the well-beloved.

Such then is the restraint that, above all else, must be practised in jesting. Thus the things most easily ridiculed are those which call for neither strong disgust nor the deepest sympathy. This is why all laughing-matters are found among those blemishes noticeable in the conduct of people who are neither objects of general esteem nor yet full of misery, and not apparently merely fit to be hurried off to execution for their crimes; and these blemishes, if deftly handled, raise laughter. In ugliness, too, and in physical blemishes there is good enough matter for jesting, but here as elsewhere the limits of licence are the main question. As to this, not only is there a rule excluding remarks made in bad taste, but also, even though you could say something with highly comical effect, an orator must avoid each of two dangers: he must not let his jesting become buffoonery or mere mimicking. ...

SOURCE: extract from *De Oratore*, translated by E. W. Sutton and H. Rackham (London, 1942): Book II, pp. 371, 373, 375.

NOTE

1. [Ed.] Democritus: the so-called 'laughing philosopher' of Abdera (c. 460–370 BC).

Evanthius   (4th century AD)

The Origins and Nature of Comedy

... Comedy is a story treating of various habits and customs of
public and private affairs, from which one may learn what is of
use in life, on the one hand, and what must be avoided, on the
other. The Greeks defined it as follows: κωμωδίαἐστὶν ἰδιωτικῶν
καὶ πολιτικῶν πραγμάτων ἀκίνδυνος περίοχή.[1] Cicero says that
comedy is 'a copy of life, a mirror of custom, a reflection of
truth'. Comedies, moreover, are so named from early custom;
since in country towns compositions of this sort were originally
played among the Greeks; as in Italy the people used to be held
at crossroads by games where a measure of speech was
introduced while the acts were being changed. Or ἀπὸ των
κωμῶν:[2] this is, from the acts of the lives of men who inhabit
country towns because of the mediocrity of the happy; not in
kingly halls, like tragic characters. Comedy, indeed, comprises
action and speech, since it is verse based upon a representation
of life and an imitation of customs. It is uncertain which of the
Greeks first invented comedy; of the Latins there is no doubt.
Livius Andronicus first invented comedy and the national
drama; he said, 'Comedy is the mirror of everyday life', nor was
this without reason. For as we gaze into a mirror we easily
perceive the features of the truth in the reflection; and so, in
reading a comedy do we easily observe the reflection of life and
of custom. ...

SOURCE: extract from *De Tragœdia et Comœdia*, attributed to
Donatus; translated by Mildred Rogers in Barratt H. Clark
(ed.), *European Theories of the Drama* (New York, 1918; revised
edition, 1929), p. 43. (On the Evanthius/Donatus attribu-
tions, see the reference to modern discussion in the Introduction, above.)

NOTES

1. [Ed.] Translation: 'Comedy is the epitome, free from danger, of private and public matters.'
2. [Ed.] Translation: 'from the villages'.

Dante Alighieri   (c. 1319)

The Distinction between Tragedy and Comedy

... The title of the work is, 'Here begins the Comedy of Dante Alighieri, a Florentine by birth but not in character'.[1] To understand the title, it must be known that comedy is derived from *comos*, 'a village', and from *oda*, 'a song'; so that a comedy is, so to speak, 'a rustic song'. Comedy, then, is a certain genre of poetic narrative differing from all others. For it differs from tragedy in its matter, in that tragedy is tranquil and conducive to wonder at the beginning, but foul and conducive to horror at the end, or catastrophe; for which reason it is derived from *tragos*, meaning 'goat', and *oda*, making it, as it were, a 'goat song'; that is, foul as a goat is foul. This is evident in Seneca's tragedies. Comedy, on the other hand, introduces a situation of adversity, but ends its matter in prosperity, as is evident in Terence's comedies. And for this reason some writers have the custom of saying in their salutations, by way of greeting, 'a tragic beginning and a comic ending to you'. And, as well, they differ in their manner of speaking. Tragedy uses an elevated and sublime style, while comedy uses an unstudied and low style. ...

SOURCE: extract from *Epistle to Can Grande*, translated by Robert S. Haller in *Literary Criticism of Dante Alighieri* (Lincoln, Nebraska, 1973), p. 100.

NOTE

1. [Ed.] The work is more generally known as *La Divina Commedia*, or *Divine Comedy*, consisting of three separate but inter-related long poems in *terza rima:* 'Hell', 'Purgatory' and 'Paradise'.

From the Renaissance
to Bergson

PART TWO

From the Renaissance
to Bergson

Nicholas Udall   (1552)

Mirth and Recreation

...

What creature is in health, either young or old,
But some mirth with modesty will be glad to use?
As we in this Interlude shall now unfold,
Wherein all scurrility we utterly refuse,
Avoiding such mirth wherein is abuse:
Knowing nothing more commendable for a man's recreation
Than Mirth which is used in an honest fashion:
For Mirth prolongeth life, and causeth health,
Mirth recreates our spirits and voideth pensiveness,
Mirth increaseth amity, not hindering our wealth,
Mirth is to be used both of more and less,
Being mixed with virtue in decent comeliness,

...

SOURCE: extract from the Prologue to *Ralph Roister Doister*
(1552); reprinted in *The Minor Elizabethan Drama*: II, *Pre-
Shakespearean Comedies* (Everyman's Library, London, 1910),
p. 3.

Sir Philip Sidney   (c. 1580)

Delight and Laughter

... our comedians think there is no delight without laughter;
which is very wrong, for though laughter may come with delight, yet cometh it not of delight, as though delight should be

the cause of laughter; but well may one thing breed both together. Nay, rather in themselves they have, as it were, a kind
of contrariety: for delight we scarcely do but in things that have
a conveniency to ourselves or to the general nature; laughter
almost ever cometh of things most disproportioned to ourselves
and nature. Delight hath a joy in it, either permanent or present.
Laughter hath only a scornful tickling. For example, we are
ravished with delight to see a fair woman, and yet are far from
being moved to laughter. We laugh at deformed creatures,
wherein certainly we cannot delight. We delight in good
chances, we laugh at mischances; we delight to hear the happiness of our friends, or country, at which he were worthy to be
laughed at that would laugh. We shall, contrarily, laugh sometimes to find a matter quite mistaken and go down the hill
against the bias, in the mouth of some such men, as for the
respect of them one shall be heartily sorry, yet he cannot choose
but laugh; and so is rather pained than delighted with laughter.
Yet deny I not but that they may go well together: for as in
Alexander's picture well set out we delight without laughter,
and in twenty mad antics we laugh without delight; so in
Hercules, painted with his great beard and furious countenance,
in woman's attire, spinning at Omphale's commandment, it
breedeth both delight and laughter. For the representing of so
strange a power in love procureth delight: and the scornfulness
of the action stirreth laughter. ...

SOURCE: extract from *An Apology for Poetry* (1595), ed. Geoffrey
Shepherd (London, 1965), p. 136.

Ben Jonson (before 1637)

Wise and Foolish Laughter

... Nor, is the moving of laughter alwaies the end of *Comedy*, that is rather a fowling for the peoples delight, or their fooling. For, as *Aristotle* saies rightly, the moving of laughter is a fault in Comedie, a kind of turpitude, that depraves some part of a mans nature without a disease. As a wry face without paine moves laughter, or a deformed vizard, or a rude Clowne, drest in a Ladies habit, and using her actions, wee dislike and scorne such representations; which made the ancient Philosophers ever thinke laughter unfitting in a wise man. And this induc'd *Plato* to esteeme of *Homer*, as a sacrilegious Person: because he presented the *Gods* sometimes laughing. As, also, it is divinely said of *Aristotle*, that to seeme ridiculous is a part of dishonesty, and foolish.

So that, what either in the words, or Sense of an Author, or in the language, or Actions of men, is a wry or depraved, doth strangely stirre meane affections, and provoke for the most part to laughter. And therefore it was cleare that all insolent, and obscene speaches; jest[s] upon the best men; injuries to particular persons; perverse, and sinister Sayings (and the rather unexpected) in the old Comedy, did move laughter; especially, where it did imitate any dishonesty; and scurrility came forth in the place of wit: which who understands the nature and *Genius* of laughter, cannot but perfectly know.

Of which *Aristophanes* affords an ample harvest, having not only outgone *Plautus*, or any other in that kinde; but express'd all the moods, and figures, of what is ridiculous, oddly. In short, as Vinegar is not accounted good, untill the wine be corrupted: so jests that are true and naturall, seldome raise laughter, with the beaste, the multitude. They love nothing, that is right, and proper. The farther it runs from reason, or possibility with them, the better it is. What could have made them laugh, like to see *Socrates* presented, that Example of all good life, honesty and

vertue, to have him hoisted up with a Pullie, and there play the
Philosopher, in a basquet? Measure, how many foote a Flea
could skip *Geometrically*, by a just Scale, and edifie the people
from the ingine? This was *Theatricall* wit, right Stage-jesting,
and relishing a Play-house, invented for scorne, and laughter;
whereas, if it had savour'd of equity, truth, perspicuity, and
Candour, to have tasten a wise, or a learned Palate, spit it out
presently; this is bitter and profitable, this instructs, and would
informe us: what needs wee know anything, that are nobly
borne, more then a Horse-race, or a hunting-match, our day to
breake with Citizens, and such innate mysteries? This is truly
leaping from the Stage to the Tumbrell againe, reducing all
witt to the original Dungcart. ...

SOURCE: extract from *Timber: or, Discoveries; Made upon Men
and Matter* (published posthumously, 1640); in Jonson's
Works, ed. C.H. Herford and P. and E. Simpson (Oxford,
1925–52): VIII (1947), pp. 643–4.

William Congreve (1695)

The Distinction between Wit and Humour

... You write to me, that you have Entertained your self two or
three days, with reading several Comedies, of several authors;
and your Observation is, that there is more of *Humour* in our
English Writers, than in any of the other Comick Poets, Ancient
or Modern. You desire to know of my Opinion, and at the same
time my Thought, of that which is generally call'd *Humour* in
Comedy.

I agree with you, in an Impartial Preference of our English
Writers, in that Particular. But if I tell you my Thoughts of
Humour, I must at the same time confess, that what I take for
true *Humour*, has not been so often written even by them, as is

generally believed: And some who valued themselves, and have been esteem'd by others, for that kind of Writing, have seldom touch'd upon it. To make this appear to the World, would require a long and labour'd Discourse, and such as I neither am able nor willing to undertake. But such little Remarks, as may be contained within the Compass of a Letter, and such unpre- meditated Thoughts, as may be Communicated between Friend and Friend, without incurring the Censure of the World, or setting up for a *Dictator*, you shall have from me, since you have enjoyn'd it.

To Define *Humour*, perhaps, were as difficult, as to Define *Wit*; for like that, it is of infinite variety. To Enumerate the several *Humours* of Men, were a Work as endless, as to sum up their several Opinions. And in my mind the *Quot homines tot Sententiæ*,[1] might have been more properly interpreted of *Humour*; since there are many Men of the same Opinion in many things, who are yet quite different in Humours. But thô we cannot certainly tell what *Wit* is, or, what *Humour* is, yet we may go near to shew something, which is not *Wit* or not *Humour*; and yet often mistaken for both. And since I have mentioned *Wit* and *Humour* together, let me make the first Distinction between them, and observe to you that *Wit is often mistaken for Humour*.

I have observed, that when a few things have been Wittily and Pleasantly spoken by any Character in a Comedy; it has been very usual for those, who make their Remarks on a Play, while it is acting, to say, *Such a thing is very Humourously spoken: There is a great Deal of Humour in that Part*. Thus the Character of the Person speaking, may be, Surprizingly and Pleasantly, is mistaken for a Character of *Humour*; which indeed is a Character of *Wit*. But there is a great Difference between a Comedy, wherein there are many things *Humorously*, as they call it, which is *Pleasantly* spoken; and one, where there are several Characters of *Humour*, distinguish'd by the Particular and Different Hu- mours, appropriated to the several Persons represented, and which naturally arise, from the different Constitutions, Com- plexions, and Dispositions of Men. The saying of Humorous Things, does not distinguish Characters; For every Person in a Comedy may be allow'd to speak them. From a Witty Man they are expected; and even a *Fool* may be permitted to stumble on them by chance. Thô I make a Difference betwixt *Wit* and *Humour*; yet I do not think that Humorous Characters exclude Wit: No, but the Manner of *Wit* should be adapted to the *Humour*. As for Instance, a Character of a Splenetick and Peevish *Humour*, should have a Satyrical Wit. A Jolly and Sanguine *Humour*, should have a Facetious Wit. The Former should speak Positively; the Latter, Carelessly: For the former Observes, and shews things as they are; the latter, rather overlooks Nature, and speaks things as he would have them; and his *Wit* and *Humour* have both of them a less Alloy of Judgment than the others.

As *Wit*, so, its opposite, *Folly, is sometimes mistaken for Humour.*

When a Poet brings a *Character* on the Stage, committing a thousand Absurdities, and talking Impertinencies, roaring Aloud, and Laughing immoderately, on every, or rather upon no occasion; this is a Character of Humour.

Is any thing more common, than to have a pretended Comedy, stuff'd with such Grotesques, Figures, and Farce Fools? Things, that either are not in Nature, or if they are, are Monsters, and Births of Mischance; and consequently as such, should be stifled, and huddled out of the way, like *Sooterkins*; that Mankind may not be shock'd with an appearing Possibility of the Degeneration of a God-like *Species*. For my part, I am as willing to Laugh, as any body, and as easily diverted with an Object truly ridiculous: but at the same time, I can never care for seeing things, that force me to entertain low thoughts of my Nature. I dont know how it is with others, but I confess freely to you, I could never look upon a Monkey, without very Mortifying Reflections; thô I never heard any thing to the Contrary, why that Creature is not Originally of a Distinct *Species*. As I dont think *Humour* exclusive of *Wit*, neither do I think it inconsistent with *Folly*; but I think the Follies should be only such, as Mens Humours may incline them to; and not Follies intirely abstracted from both Humour and Nature.

Sometimes, *Personal Defects are misrepresented for Humours.*

I mean, sometimes Characters are barbarously exposed on the Stage, ridiculing Natural Deformities, Casual Defects in the Senses, and Infirmities of Age. Sure the Poet must both be very Ill-natur'd himself, and think his Audience so, when he proposes by shewing a Man Deform'd, or Deaf, or Blind, to give them an agreeable Entertainment; and hopes to raise their Mirth, by what is truly an object of Compassion. But much need not be said upon this Head to any body, especially to you, who in one of your Letters to me concerning Mr *Johnson's Fox*,[2] have justly excepted against this Immoral part of *Ridicule* in *Corbaccio's* Character; and there I must agree with you to blame him, whom otherwise I cannot enough admire, for his great Mastery of true Humour in Comedy.

Exteranl Habit of Body is often mistaken for Humour.

By *External Habit*, I do not mean the Ridiculous Dress or Cloathing of a Character, thô that goes a good way in some received Characters. (But undoubtedly a Man's Humour may incline him to dress differently from other People) But I mean a Singularity of Manners, Speech, and Behaviour, peculiar to all, or most of the same Country, Trade, Profession, or Education. I cannot think, that a *Humour*, which is only a Habit, or Disposition contracted by Use or Custom; for by a Disuse, or Complyance with other Customs, it may be worn off, or diversify'd.

Affectation is generally mistaken for Humour.

These are indeed so much alike, that at a Distance, they may be mistaken one for the other. For what is *Humour* in one, may be *Affectation* in another; and nothing is more common, than for some to affect particular ways of saying, and doing things, peculiar to others, whom they admire and would imitate. *Humour* is the Life, *Affectation* the Picture. He that draws a Character of *Affectation*, shews *Humour* at the Second Hand; he at best but publishes a Translation, and his Pictures are but Copies.

But as these two last distinctions are the Nicest, so it may be most proper to Explain them, by Particular Instances from some Author of Reputation. *Humour* I take, either to be born with us, and so of a Natural Growth; or else to be grafted into us, by some accidental change in the Constitution, or revolution of the Internal Habit of Body; by which it becomes, if I may so call it, Naturaliz'd. ...

SOURCE: extract from *A Letter to John Dennis, concerning Humour in Comedy* (10 July 1695); reproduced in John C. Hodges (ed.), *William Congreve: Letters and Documents* (London, 1964), pp. 176–80.

NOTES

1. [Ed.] Trans: 'As many opinions as there are people', from Terence's *Phormio* (I 454).
2. [Ed.] I.e., Ben Jonson's *Volpone*.

Henry Fielding   (1742)

Affectation and the Ridiculous

... Now, a comic romance is a comic epic poem in prose; differing from comedy, as the serious epic from tragedy: its action being more extended and comprehensive; containing a much larger circle of incidents, and introducing a greater variety of characters. It differs from the serious romance in its fable and action, in this; that, as in the one these are grave and solemn, so in the other they are light and ridiculous; it differs in its characters by introducing persons of inferior rank, and consequently, of inferior manners, whereas the grave romance sets the highest before us: lastly, in its sentiments and diction; by preserving the ludicrous instead of the sublime. In the diction, I think, burlesque itself may be sometimes admitted; of which many instances will occur in this work, as in the description of the battles, and some other places, not necessary to be pointed out to the classical reader, for whose entertainment those parodies or burlesque imitations are chiefly calculated.

But though we have sometimes admitted this in our diction, we have carefully excluded it from our sentiments and characters; for there it is never properly introduced, unless in writings of the burlesque kind, which this is not intended to be. Indeed, no two species of writing can differ more widely than the comic and the burlesque; for as the latter is ever the exhibition of what is monstrous and unnatural, and where our delight, if we examine it, arises from the surprizing absurdity, as in appropriating the manners of the highest to the lowest, or *è converso*; so in the former we should ever confine ourselves strictly to nature, from the just imitation of which will flow all the pleasure we can this way convey to a sensible reader. And perhaps there is one reason why a comic writer should of all others be the least excused for deviating from nature, since it may not be always so easy for a serious poet to meet with the great and the admirable; but life everywhere furnishes an accurate observer with the ridiculous.

I have hinted this little concerning burlesque, because I have often heard that name given to performances which have been truly of the comic kind, from the author's having sometimes admitted it in his diction only; which, as it is the dress of poetry, doth, like the dress of men, establish characters (the one of the whole poem, and the other of the whole man), in vulgar opinion, beyond any of their greater excellences: but surely, a certain drollery in stile, where characters and sentiments are perfectly natural, no more constitutes the burlesque, than an empty pomp and dignity of words, where everything else is mean and low, can entitle any performance to the appellation of the true sublime.

And I apprehend my Lord Shaftesbury's opinion of mere burlesque agrees with mine, when he asserts, There is no such thing to be found in the writings of the ancients. But perhaps I have less abhorrence than he professes for it; and that, not because I have had some little success on the stage this way, but rather as it contributes more to exquisite mirth and laughter than any other; and these are probably more wholesome physic for the mind, and conduce better to purge away spleen, melancholy, and ill affections, than is generally imagined. Nay, I will appeal to common observation, whether the same companies are not found more full of good-humour and benevolence, after they have been sweetened for two or three hours with entertainment of this kind, than when soured by a tragedy or a grave lecture.

But to illustrate all this by another science, in which, perhaps,

we shall see the distinction more clearly and plainly, let us
examine the works of a comic history painter, with those performances which the Italians call Caricatura, where we shall
find the true excellence of the former to consist in the exactest
copying of nature; insomuch that a judicious eye instantly re-
jects anything *outré*, any liberty which the painter hath taken
with the features of that *alma mater*; whereas in the Caricatura
we allow all licence – its aim is to exhibit monsters, not men;
and all distortions and exaggerations whatever are within its
proper province.

Now, what Caricatura is in painting, Burlesque is in writing;
and in the same manner the comic writer and painter correlate
to each other. And here I shall observe, that, as in the former
the painter seems to have the advantage; so it is in the latter
infinitely on the side of the writer; for the Monstrous is much
easier to paint than describe, and the Ridiculous to describe
than paint.

And though perhaps this latter species doth not in either
science so strongly affect and agitate the muscles as the other;
yet it will be owned, I believe, that a more rational and useful
pleasure arises to us from it. He who should call the ingenious
Hogarth a burlesque painter, would, in my opinion, do him
very little honour; for sure it is much easier, much less the
subject of admiration, to paint a man with a nose, or any other
feature, of a preposterous size, or to expose him in some absurd
or monstrous attitude, than to express the affections of men on
canvas. It hath been thought a vast commendation of a painter
to say his figures seem to breathe; but surely it is a much greater
and nobler applause, that they appear to think.

But to return. The Ridiculous only, as I have before said, falls
within my province in the present work. Nor will some explanation of this word be thought impertinent by the reader, if he
considers how wonderfully it hath been mistaken, even by
writers who have professed it; for to what but such a mistake
can we attribute the many attempts to ridicule the blackest
villanies, and, what is yet worse, the most dreadful calamities?
What could exceed the absurdity of an author, who should
write the comedy of Nero, with the merry incident of ripping
up his mother's belly? or what would give a greater shock to

humanity than an attempt to expose the miseries of poverty and distress to ridicule? And yet the reader will not want much learning to suggest such instances to himself.

Besides, it may seem remarkable, that Aristotle, who is so fond and free of definitions, hath not thought proper to define the Ridiculous. Indeed, where he tells us it is proper to comedy, he hath remarked that villainy is not its object: but he hath not, as I remember, positively asserted what is. Nor doth the Abbé Bellegarde, who hath written a treatise on this subject, though he shows us many species of it, once trace it to its fountain.[1]

The only source of the true Ridiculous (as it appears to me) is affectation. But though it arises from one spring only, when we consider the infinite streams into which this one branches, we shall presently cease to admire the copious field it affords to an observer. Now, affectation proceeds from one of these two causes, vanity or hypocrisy: for as vanity puts us on affecting false characters, in order to purchase applause; so hypocrisy sets us on an endeavour to avoid censure, by concealing our vices, under an appearance of their opposite virtues. And though these two causes are often confounded (for there is some difficulty in distinguishing them), yet as they proceed from very different motives, so they are as clearly distinct in their operations: for indeed, the affectation which arises from vanity is nearer to truth than the other, as it hath not that violent repugnancy of nature to struggle with, which that of the hypocrite hath. It may be likewise noted, that affectation doth not imply an absolute negation of those qualities which are affected; and, therefore, though, when it proceeds from hypocrisy, it be nearly allied to deceit; yet when it comes from vanity only, it partakes of the nature of ostentation: for instance, the affectation of liberality in a vain man differs visibly from the same affectation in the avaricious; for though the vain man is not what he would appear, or hath not the virtue he affects, to the degree he would be thought to have it; yet it sits less awkwardly on him than on the avaricious man, who is the very reverse of what he would seem to be.

From the discovery of this affectation arises the Ridiculous, which always strikes the reader with surprize and pleasure; and that in a higher and stronger degree when the affectation arises from hypocrisy, than when from vanity; for to discover any one to be the exact reverse of what he affects, is more surprizing, and consequently more ridiculous, than to find him a little deficient in the quality he desires the reputation of. I might observe that our Ben Jonson, who of all men understood the Ridiculous the best, hath chiefly used the hypocritical affectation.

Now, from affectation only, the misfortunes and calamities of life, or the imperfections of nature, may become the objects of ridicule. Surely he hath a very ill-framed mind who can look on ugliness, infirmity, or poverty, as ridiculous in themselves: nor do I believe any man living, who meets a dirty fellow riding through the streets in a cart, is struck with an idea of the Ridiculous from it; but if he should see the same figure descend from his coach and six, or bolt from his chair with his hat under his arm, he would then begin to laugh, and with justice. In the same manner, were we to enter a poor house and behold a wretched family shivering with cold and languishing with hunger, it would not incline us to laughter (at least we must have very diabolical natures if it would); but should we discover there a grate, instead of coals, adorned with flowers, empty plate or china dishes on the side-board, or any other affectation of riches and finery, either on their persons or in their furniture, we might then indeed be excused for ridiculing so fantastical an appearance. Much less are natural imperfections the object of derision; but when ugliness aims at the applause of beauty, or lameness endeavours to display agility, it is then that these unfortunate circumstances, which at first moved our compassion, tend only to raise our mirth. ...

SOURCE: extract from Author's Preface to *Joseph Andrews* (1742); reproduced in W.E. Henley (ed.), *The Complete Works of Henry Fielding* (London, 1903): i, pp. *xxx–xxxvi*.

NOTE

1. Jean-Baptiste Morvau de Bellegarde (1648–1734), *Réflexions sur le ridicule et sur les moyens de l'éviter* (1696).

Oliver Goldsmith   (1773)

A Comparison between Laughing and Sentimental Comedy

The Theatre, like all other amusements, has its Fashions and its Prejudices; and when satiated with its excellence, Mankind begin to mistake Change for Improvement. For some years, Tragedy was the reigning entertainment; but of late it has entirely given way to Comedy, and our best efforts are now exerted in these lighter kinds of composition. The pompous Train, the swelling Phrase, and the unnatural Rant, are displaced for that natural portrait of Human Folly and Frailty, of which all are judges, because all have sat for the picture.

But as in describing Nature it is presented with a double face, either of mirth or sadness, our modern Writers find themselves at a loss which chiefly to copy from; and it is now debated, Whether the Exhibition of Human Distress is likely to afford the mind more Entertainment than that of Human Absurdity?

Comedy is defined by Aristotle to be a picture of the Frailties of the lower part of Mankind, to distinguish it from Tragedy, which is an exhibition of the Misfortunes of the Great. When Comedy therefore ascends to produce the Characters of Princes or Generals upon the Stage, it is out of its walk, since Low Life and Middle Life are entirely its object. The principal question therefore is, Whether in describing Low or Middle Life, an exhibition of its Follies be not preferable to a detail of its Calamities? Or in other words, Which deserves the preference? The Weeping Sentimental Comedy so much in fashion at present, or the Laughing and even Low Comedy, which seems to have been last exhibited by Vanburgh and Cibber?

If we apply to authorities, all the Great Masters in the Dramatic Art have but one opinion. Their rule is, that as Tragedy displays the Calamities of the Great; so Comedy should excite our laughter by ridiculously exhibiting the Follies of the Lower Part of Mankind. Boileau, one of the best modern Critics, asserts, that Comedy will not admit of Tragic Distress.

Le Comique, ennemi des soupirs et des pleurs,
N'admet point dans ses vers de tragiques douleurs.[1]

Nor is this rule without the strongest foundation in Nature, as the distresses of the Mean by no means affect us so strongly as the Calamities of the Great. When Tragedy exhibits to us some Great Man fallen from his height, and struggling with want and adversity, we feel his situation in the same manner as we suppose he himself must feel, our pity is increased in proportion to the height from whence he fell. On the contrary, we do not so strongly sympathize with one born in humbler circumstances, and encountering accidental distress: so that while we melt for Belisarius, we scarce give halfpence to the Beggar who accosts us in the street. The one has our pity; the other our contempt. Distress, therefore, is the proper object of Tragedy, since the Great excite our pity by their fall; but not equally so of Comedy, since the Actors employed in it are originally so mean, that they sink but little by their fall.

Since the first origin of the Stage, Tragedy and Comedy have run in different channels, and never till of late encroached upon the provinces of each other. Terence, who seems to have made the nearest approaches, yet always judiciously stops short before he comes to the downright pathetic; and yet he is even reproached by Cæsar for wanting the *vis comica*. All the other Comic Writers of antiquity aim only at rendering Folly or Vice ridiculous, but never exalt their characters into buskined pomp, or make what Voltaire humourously calls a *Tradesman's Tragedy*.

Yet, notwithstanding this weight of authority, and the universal practice of former ages, a new species of Dramatic Composition has been introduced under the name of *Sentimental* Comedy, in which the virtues of Private Life are exhibited, rather than the Vices exposed; and the Distresses, rather than the Faults of Mankind, make our interest in the piece. These Comedies have had of late great success, perhaps from their novelty, and also from their flattering every man in his favourite foible. In these Plays almost all the Characters are good, and exceedingly generous; they are lavish enough of their *Tin* Money on the Stage, and though they want Humour, have abundance of Sentiment and Feeling. If they happen to have

Faults or Foibles, the Spectator is taught not only to pardon, but to applaud them, in consideration of the goodness of their hearts, so that Folly, instead of being ridiculed, is commended, and the Comedy aims at touching our Passions without the power of being truly pathetic: in this manner we are likely to lose one great source of Entertainment on the Stage; for while the Comic Poet is invading the province of the Tragic Muse, he leaves her lovely Sister quite neglected. Of this, however, he is noway solicitous, as he measures his fame by his profits.

But it will be said, that the Theatre is formed to amuse Mankind, and that it matters little, if this end be answered, by what means it is obtained. If Mankind find delight in weeping at Comedy, it would be cruel to abridge them in that or any other innocent pleasure. If those Pieces are denied the name of Comedies; yet call them by any other name, and if they are delightful, they are good. Their success, it will be said, is a mark of their merit, and it is only abridging our happiness to deny us an inlet to Amusement.

These objections, however, are rather specious than solid. It is true, that Amusement is a great object of the Theatre; and it will be allowed, that these Sentimental Pieces do often amuse us: but the question is, Whether the True Comedy would not amuse us more? The question is, Whether a Character supported throughout a Piece with its Ridicule still attending, would not give us more delight than this species of Bastard Tragedy, which only is applauded because it is new?

A friend of mine who was sitting unmoved at one of these Sentimental Pieces, was asked, how he could be so indifferent. 'Why, truly', says he, 'as the Hero is but a Tradesman, it is indifferent to me whether he be turned out of his Counting-House on Fish-street Hill, since he will still have enough left to open shop in St Giles's.'

The other objection is as ill-grounded; for though we should give these Pieces another name, it will not mend their efficacy. It will continue a kind of *mulish* production, with all the defects of its opposite parents, and marked with sterility. If we are permitted to make Comedy weep, we have an equal right to make Tragedy laugh, and to set down in Blank Verse the Jests and Repartees of all the Attendants in a Funeral Procession.

But there is one Argument in favour of Sentimental Comedy which will keep it on the Stage in spite of all that can be said against it. It is, of all others, the most easily written. Those abilities that can hammer out a Novel, are fully sufficient for the production of a Sentimental Comedy. It is only sufficient to raise the Characters a little, to deck out the Hero with a Ribband, or give the Heroine a Title; then to put an Insipid Dialogue, without Character or Humour, into their mouths, give them mighty good hearts, very fine cloaths, furnish a new sett of Scenes, make a Pathetic Scene or two, with a sparkling of tender melancholy Conversation through the whole, and there is no doubt but all the Ladies will cry, and all the Gentlemen applaud.

Humour at present seems to be departing from the Stage, and it will soon happen, that our Comic Players will have nothing left for it but a fine Coat and a Song. It depends upon the Audience whether they will actually drive those poor Merry Creatures from the Stage, or sit at a Play as gloomy as at the Tabernacle. It is not easy to recover an art when once lost; and it would be but a just punishment that when, by our being too fastidious, we have banished Humour from the Stage, we should ourselves be deprived of the art of Laughing. ...

SOURCE: extract from *An Essay on the Theatre; or A Comparison between Laughing and Sentimental Comedy* (1773); reproduced in Arthur Friedman (ed.), *The Collected Works of Oliver Goldsmith*, 5 vols (Oxford, 1966): III, pp. 209–13.

NOTE

1. [Ed.] Boileau, *L'Art Poétique* (1674): chant III, 401–2.

William Hazlitt (1819)

Modern Manners Fatal to Comedy

The question which has been often asked, *Why there are compara-tively so few good modern Comedies?* appears in a great measure to answer itself. It is because so many excellent comedies have been written, that there are none written at present. Comedy naturally wears itself out – destroys the very food on which it lives; and by constantly and successfully exposing the follies and weaknesses of mankind to ridicule, in the end leaves itself with nothing worth laughing at. It holds the mirror up to nature; and men, seeing their most striking peculiarities and defects pass in gay review before them, learn either to avoid or conceal them. It is not the criticism which the public taste exercises upon the stage, but the criticism which the stage exercises upon public manners, that is fatal to comedy, by rendering the subject-matter of it tame, correct and spiritless. We are drilled into a sort of stupid decorum, and forced to wear the same dull uniform of outward appearance; and yet it is asked, why the Comic Muse does not point, as she was wont, at the peculiarities of our gait and gesture, and exhibit the picturesque contrasts of our dress and costume, in all that graceful variety in which she delights. The genuine source of comic writing,

> Where it must live, or have no life at all,

is undoubtedly to be found in the distinguishing peculiarities of men and manners. Now this distinction can subsist, so as to be strong, pointed, and general, only while the manners of different classes are formed almost immediately by their particular cir-cumstances, and the characters of individuals by their natural temperament and situation, without being everlastingly modi-fied and neutralized by intercourse with the world – by know-ledge and education. In a certain stage of society, men may be said to vegetate like trees, and to become rooted to the soil in which they grow. They have no idea of any thing beyond themselves and their immediate sphere of action; they are, as it were, circumscribed and defined by their particular circumstances; they are what their situation makes them, and nothing more. Each is absorbed in his own profession or pursuit, and each in his turn contracts that habitual peculiarity of manners and opinions which makes him the subject of ridicule to others, and the sport of the Comic Muse. Thus the physician is nothing but a physician, the lawyer a mere lawyer, the scholar degenerates into a pedant, the country squire is a different species of being from the fine gentleman, the citizen and the courtier inhabit a different world, and even the affectation of certain characters, in aping the follies or vices of their betters, only serves to shew the immeasurable distance which custom or fortune has placed between them. Hence the earlier comic writers, taking advantage of this mixed and solid mass of ignorance, folly, pride, and prejudice, made those deep and lasting incisions into it, – have given those sharp and nice touches, that bold relief to their characters, – have opposed them in every variety of contrast and collision, of conscious self-satisfaction and mutual antipathy, with a power which can only find full scope in the same rich and inexhaustible materials. But in proportion as comic genius succeeds in taking off the mask from ignorance and conceit, it teaches us

To see ourselves as others see us, –

in proportion as we are brought out on the stage together, and our prejudices clash one against the other, our sharp angular points wear off; we are no longer rigid in absurdity, passionate in folly, and we prevent the ridicule directed at our habitual foibles by laughing at them ourselves.

If it be said, that there is the same fund of absurdity and prejudice in the world as ever – that there are the same unaccountable perversities lurking at the bottom of every breast, – I should answer, Be it so: but at least we keep our follies to ourselves as much as possible; we palliate, shuffle, and equivocate with them; they sneak into bye-corners, and do not, like Chaucer's *Canterbury Pilgrims*, march along the high road and form a procession; they do not entrench themselves strongly behind custom and precedent; they are not embodied in professions and ranks in life; they are not organized into a system; they do not openly resort to a standard, but are a sort of straggling non-descripts, that, like *Wart*, 'present no mark to the foeman'. As to the gross and palpable absurdities of modern manners, they are too shallow and barefaced, and those who affect them are too little *serious* in them, to make them worth the detection of the Comic Muse. They proceed from an idle, impudent affectation of folly in general, in the dashing *bravura* style, not from an infatuation with any of its characteristic modes. In short, the proper object of ridicule is *egotism*: and a man cannot be a very great egotist, who every day sees himself represented on the stage. We are deficient in comedy, because we are without characters in real life – as we have no historical pictures, because we have no faces proper for them. ...

SOURCE: extract from 'On the Comic Writers of the Last Century', in *Lectures on the English Comic Writers* (1819); reproduced in P.P. Howe (ed.), *The Complete Works of William Hazlitt*, (London, 1931): VI, pp. 149–51.

Charles Lamb   (1822)

The Importance of Not Being Earnest

The artificial Comedy, or Comedy of manners, is quite extinct on our stage. Congreve and Farquhar show their heads once in seven years only, to be exploded and put down instantly. The times cannot bear them. Is it for a few wild speeches, an occasional licence of dialogue? I think not altogether. The business of their dramatic characters will not stand the moral test. We screw everything up to that. Idle gallantry in a fiction, a dream, the passing pageant of an evening, startles us in the same way as the alarming indications of profligacy in a son or ward in real life should startle a parent or guardian. We have no such middle emotions as dramatic interests left. We see a stage libertine playing his loose pranks of two hours' duration, and of no after consequence, with the severe eyes which inspect real vices with their bearings upon two worlds. We are spectators to a plot or intrigue (not reducible in life to the point of strict morality) and take it all for truth. We substitute a real for a dramatic person, and judge him accordingly. We try him in our courts, from which there is no appeal to the *dramatis personae*, his peers. We have been spoiled with – not sentimental comedy – but a tyrant far more pernicious to our pleasures which has succeeded to it; the exclusive and all devouring drama of common life; where the moral point is every thing; where, instead of the fictitious half-believed personages of the stage (the phantoms of the old comedy) we recognise ourselves, our brothers, aunts, with an interest in what is going on so hearty and substantial, that we cannot afford our moral judgment, in its deepest and most vital results, to compromise or slumber for a moment. What is *there* transacting, by no modification is made to affect us in any other manner than the same events or characters would do in our relationships of life. We carry our fire-side concerns to the theatre with us. We do not go thither, like our ancestors, to escape from the pressure of reality, so much as to confirm our experience of it; to make assurance double, and take a bond of fate. We must live our toilsome lives twice over, as it was the mournful privilege of Ulysses to descend twice to the shades. All that neutral ground of character, which stood between vice and virtue; or which in fact was indifferent to neither, where neither properly was called in question; that happy breathing-place from the burden of a perpetual moral questioning – the sanctuary and quiet Alsatia of hunted casuistry – is broken up and disfranchised, as injurious to the interests of society. The privileges of the place are taken away by law. We dare not dally with images, or names, of wrong. We bark like foolish dogs at shadows. We dread infection from the scenic representation of disorder; and fear a painted pustule. In our anxiety that our morality should not take cold, we wrap it up in a great blanket surtout of precaution against the breeze and sunshine.

I confess for myself that (with no great delinquencies to answer for) I am glad for a season to take an airing beyond the diocese of the strict conscience, – not to live always in the precincts of the law-courts – but now and then, for a dream-while or so, to imagine a world with no meddling restrictions – to get into recesses, whither the hunter cannot follow me –

> Secret shades
> Of woody Ida's inmost grove
> Where yet there was no fear of Jove.

I come back to my cage and my restraint the fresher and more healthy for it. I wear my shackles more contentedly for having respired the breath of an imaginary freedom. I do not know how it is with others, but I feel the better always for perusal of one of Congreve's – nay, why should I not add even of Wycherley's – comedies. I am the gayer at least for it; and I could never connect those sports of a witty fancy in any shape with any result to be drawn from them to imitation in real life. They are a world of themselves almost as much as fairy land. Take one of their characters male or female (with a few exceptions they are alike), and place it in a modern play, and my virtuous indignation shall rise against the profligate wretch as warmly as the Catos of the pit could desire; because in a modern play I am to judge of the right and the wrong. The standard of *police* is the measure of *political justice*. The atmosphere will blight it, it cannot live here. It has got into a moral world, where it has no business, from which it must needs fall headlong; as dizzy, and incapable of making a stand, as a Swedenborgian bad spirit that has wandered unawares into the sphere of one of his Good Men or Angels. But in its own world do we feel the creature is so very bad? The Fainalls and the Mirabels,[1] the Dorimants and the Lady Touchwoods, in their own sphere, do not offend my moral sense; in fact they do not appeal to it at all. They seem engaged in their proper element. They break through no laws, or conscious restraints. They know of none. They have got out of Christendom into the land – what shall I call it? – of cuckoldry – the Utopia of gallantry, where pleasure is a duty, and the manners perfect freedom. It is altogether a speculative scene of things, which has no reference whatever to the world that is. No good person can justly be offended as a spectator, because no good person suffers on the stage. Judged morally, every charac-

ter in these plays – the few exceptions only are *mistakes* – is alike
essentially vain and worthless. The great art of Congreve is
especially shown in this, that he has entirely excluded from his
scenes, – some little generosities on the part of Angelica perhaps
excepted, – not only anything like a faultless character, but any
pretensions to goodness or good feelings whatsoever. Whether
he did this designedly, or instinctively, the effect is as happy, as
the design (if design) was bold. I used to wonder at the strange
power which his *Way of the World* in particular possesses of
interesting you all along in the pursuits of characters, for whom
you absolutely care nothing – for you neither hate nor love his
personages – and I think it is owing to this very indifference for
any, that you endure the whole. He has spread a privation of
moral light, I will call it, rather than by the ugly name of
palpable darkness, over his creations; and his shadows flit before
you without distinction or preference. Had he introduced a
good character, a single gush of moral feeling, a revulsion of the
judgment to actual life and actual duties, the impertinent
Goshen would have only lighted to the discovery of deformities,
which now are none, because we think them none.

Translated into real life, the characters of his, and his friend
Wycherley's dramas, are profligates and strumpets – the business of their brief existence, the undivided pursuit of lawless
gallantry. No other spring of action, or possible motive of conduct, is recognised; principles which, universally acted upon,
must reduce this frame of things to a chaos. But we do them
wrong in so translating them. No such effects are produced in
their world. When we are among them, we are amongst a chaotic
people. We are not to judge them by our usages. No reverend
institutions are insulted by their proceedings, – for they have
none among them. No peace of families is violated – for no
family ties exist among them. No purity of the marriage bed is
stained, – for none is supposed to have a being. No deep affections are disquieted, – no holy wedlock bands are snapped
asunder, – for affection's depth and wedded faith are not of the
growth of that soil. There is neither right nor wrong, – gratitude
or its opposite, – claim or duty, – paternity or sonship. Of what
consequence is it to virtue, or how is she at all concerned about
it, whether Sir Simon, or Dapperwit, steal away Miss Martha;

or who is the father of Lord Froth's, or Sir Paul Pliant's children?

The whole is a passing pageant, where we should sit as unconcerned at the issues, for life or death, as at a battle of the frogs and mice. But, like Don Quixote, we take part against the puppets, and quite as impertinently. We dare not contemplate an Atlantis, a scheme, out of which our coxcombical moral sense is for a little transitory ease excluded. We have not the courage to imagine a state of things for which there is neither reward nor punishment. We cling to the painful necessities of shame and blame. We would indict our very dreams. ...

SOURCE: extract from 'On the Artificial Comedy of the Last Century' (1822), included in *Essays of Elia* (1823); reproduced in William Macdonald (ed.), *The Works of Charles Lamb* (London, 1903): I, pp. 281–6.

NOTE

1. [Ed.] Lamb's spelling – Mirabel, for Mirabell – is here retained.

George Meredith (1877)

(i) Comedy and Cultivated Society

... There are plain reasons why the Comic poet is not a frequent apparition; and why the great Comic poet remains without a fellow. A society of cultivated men and women is required, wherein ideas are current and the perceptions quick, that he may be supplied with matter and an audience. The semi-barbarism of merely giddy communities, and feverish emotional periods, repel him; and also a state of marked social inequality of the sexes; nor can he whose business is to address the mind be understood where there is not a moderate degree of intellectual activity.

Moreover, to touch and kindle the mind through laughter, demands more than sprightliness, a most subtle delicacy. That must be a natal gift in the Comic poet. The substance he deals with will show him a startling exhibition of the dyer's hand, if he is without it. People are ready to surrender themselves to witty thumps on the back, breast, and sides; all except the head: and it is there that he aims. He must be subtle to penetrate. A corresponding acuteness must exist to welcome him. The necessity for the two conditions will explain how it is that we count him during centuries in the singular number. ...

(ii)   The Clear-Sighted Heroines of Comedy

... The heroines of Comedy are like women of the world, not necessarily heartless from being clear-sighted: they seem so to the sentimentally-reared only for the reason that they use their wits, and are not wandering vessels crying out for a captain or a pilot. Comedy is an exhibition of their battle with men, and that of men with them: and as the two, however divergent, both look on one object, namely, Life, the gradual similarity of their impressions must bring them to some resemblance. The Comic poet dares to show us men and women coming to this mutual likeness; he is for saying that when they draw together in social life their minds grow liker; just as the philosopher discerns the similarity of boy and girl, until the girl is marched away to the nursery. Philosopher and Comic poet are of a cousinship in the eye they cast on life: and they are equally unpopular with our wilful English of the hazy region and the ideal that is not to be disturbed.

Thus, for want of instruction in the Comic idea, we lose a large audience among our cultivated middle class that we should expect to support Comedy. The sentimentalist is as averse as the Puritan and as the Bacchanalian. ...

(iii)   Comedy and the Equality of the Sexes

... But there never will be civilisation where Comedy is not possible; and that comes of some degree of social equality of the sexes. I am not quoting the Arab to exhort and disturb the somnolent East; rather for cultivated women to recognise that the Comic Muse is one of their best friends. They are blind to their interests in swelling the ranks of the sentimentalists. Let them look with their clearest vision abroad and at home. They will see that where they have no social freedom, Comedy is absent: where they are household drudges, the form of Comedy is primitive: where they are tolerably independent, but uncultivated, exciting melodrama takes its place and a sentimental version of them. Yet the Comic will out, as they would know if they listened to some of the private conversation of men whose minds are undirected by the Comic Muse: as the sentimental man, to his astonishment, would know likewise, if he in similar fashion could receive a lesson. But where women are on the road to an equal footing with men, in attainments and in liberty – in what they have won for themselves, and what has been granted them by a fair civilisation – there, and only waiting to be transplanted from life to the stage, or the novel, or the poem, pure Comedy flourishes, and is, as it would help them to be, the sweetest of diversions, the wisest of delightful companions.

Now, to look about us in the present time, I think it will be acknowledged that in neglecting the cultivation of the Comic idea, we are losing the aid of a powerful auxiliar. You see Folly perpetually sliding into new shapes in a society possessed of wealth and leisure, with many whims, many strange ailments and strange doctors. Plenty of common-sense is in the world to thrust her back when she pretends to empire. But the first-born of common-sense, the vigilant Comic, which is the genius of thoughtful laughter, which would readily extinguish her at the outset, is not serving as a public advocate.

You will have noticed the disposition of common-sense, under pressure of some pertinacious piece of light-headedness, to grow impatient and angry. That is a sign of the absence, or at least of the dormancy, of the Comic idea. For Folly is the natural prey of the Comic, known to it in all her transformations, in every disguise; and it is with the springing delight of hawk over heron, hound after fox, that it gives her chase, never fretting, never tiring, sure of having her, allowing her no rest.

Contempt is a sentiment that cannot be entertained by comic intelligence. What is it but an excuse to be idly minded, or personally lofty, or comfortably narrow, not perfectly humane? If we do not feign when we say that we despise Folly, we shut the brain. There is a disdainful attitude in the presence of Folly, partaking of the foolishness to Comic perception: and anger is not much less foolish than disdain. The struggle we have to conduct is essence against essence. Let no one doubt of the sequel when this emanation of what is firmest in us is launched to strike down the daughter of Unreason and Sentimentalism: such being Folly's parentage, when it is respectable. ...

(iv) The Humour of the Mind

... Incidents of a kind casting ridicule on our unfortunate nature instead of our conventional life, provoke derisive laughter, which thwarts the Comic idea. But derision is foiled by the play of the intellect. Most of doubtful causes in contest are open to Comic interpretation, and any intellectual pleading of a doubtful cause contains germs of an Idea of Comedy.

The laughter of satire is a blow in the back or the face. The laughter of Comedy is impersonal and of unrivalled politeness, nearer a smile; often no more than a smile. It laughs through the mind, for the mind directs it; and it might be called the humour of the mind.

One excellent test of the civilisation of a country, as I have said, I take to be the flourishing of the Comic idea and Comedy; and the test of true Comedy is that it shall awaken thoughtful laughter.

If you believe that our civilisation is founded in commonsense (and it is the first condition of sanity to believe it), you will, when contemplating men, discern a Spirit overhead; not more heavenly than the light flashed upward from glassy surfaces, but luminous and watchful; never shooting beyond them, nor lagging in the rear; so closely attached to them that it may be taken for a slavish reflex, until its features are studied. It has the sage's brows, and the sunny malice of a faun lurks at the corners of the half-closed lips drawn in an idle wariness of half tension. That slim feasting smile, shaped like the long-bow, was once a big round Satyr's laugh, that flung up the brows like a fortress lifted by gunpowder. The laugh will come again, but it will be of the order of the smile, finely tempered, showing sunlight of the mind, mental richness rather than noisy enormity. Its common aspect is one of unsolicitous observation, as if surveying a full field and having leisure to dart on its chosen morsels, without any flattering eagerness. Men's future upon earth does not attract it; their honesty and shapeliness does; and whenever they wax out of proportion, overblown, affected, pretentious, bombastical, hypocritical, pedantic, fantastically delicate; whenever it sees them self-deceived or hoodwinked, given to run riot in idolatries, drifting into vanities, congregating in absurdities, planning short-sightedly, plotting dementedly; whenever they are at variance with their professions, and violate the unwritten but perceptible laws binding them in consideration one to another; whenever they offend sound reason, fair justice; are false in humility or mined with conceit, individually, or in the bulk – the Spirit overhead will look humanely malign and cast an oblique light on them, followed by volleys of silvery laughter. That is the Comic Spirit.

SOURCE: extracts from 'On the Idea of Comedy and the Uses of the Comic Spirit', a lecture delivered at the London Institution, 1 February 1877, and subsequently published as *An Essay on Comedy and the Uses of the Comic Spirit* (1897); reproduced in *The Works of George Meredith* (London, 1919): VII, pp. 7–9, 29–30, 60–3, 87–90.

Henri Bergson   (1899)

A Certain Rigidity of Body, Mind and Character

... What life and society require of each of us is a constantly
alert attention that discerns the outlines of the present situation,
together with a certain elasticity of mind and body to enable us
to adapt ourselves in consequence. *Tension* and *elasticity* are two
forces, mutually complementary, which life brings into play. If
these two forces are lacking in the body to any considerable
extent, we have sickness and infirmity and accidents of every
kind. If they are lacking in the mind, we find every degree of
mental deficiency, every variety of insanity. Finally, if they
are lacking in the character, we have cases of the gravest in-
adaptability to social life, which are the sources of misery
and at times the causes of crime. Once these elements of inferiority that affect the serious side of existence are removed – and
they tend to eliminate themselves in what has been called the
struggle for life – the person can live, and that in common with
other persons. But society asks for something more; it is not
satisfied with simply living, it insists on living well. What it now
has to dread is that each one of us, content with paying attention
to what affects the essentials of life, will, so far as the rest is
concerned, give way to the easy automatism of acquired habits.
Another thing it must fear is that the members of whom it is
made up, instead of aiming after an increasingly delicate adjustment of wills which will fit more and more perfectly into one
another, will confine themselves to respecting simply the fundamental conditions of this adjustment: a cut-and-dried agreement among the persons will not satisfy it, it insists on a constant
striving after reciprocal adaptation. Society will therefore be
suspicious of all *inelasticity* of character, of mind and even of
body, because it is the possible sign of a slumbering activity as
well as of an activity with separatist tendencies, that inclines to
swerve from the common centre round which society gravitates:
in short, because it is the sign of an eccentricity. And yet, society

cannot intervene at this stage by material repression, since it is not affected in a material fashion. It is confronted with something that makes it uneasy, but only as a symptom – scarcely a threat, at the very most a gesture. A gesture, therefore, will be its reply. Laughter must be something of this kind, a sort of *social gesture*. By the fear which it inspires, it restrains eccentricity, keeps constantly awake and in mutual contact certain activities of a secondary order which might retire into their shell and go to sleep, and, in short, softens down whatever the surface of the social body may retain of mechanical inelasticity. Laughter, then, does not belong to the province of esthetics alone, since unconsciously (and even immorally in many particular instances) it pursues a utilitarian aim of general improvement. And yet there is something esthetic about it, since the comic comes into being just when society and the individual, freed from the worry of self-preservation, begin to regard themselves as works of art. In a word, if a circle be drawn round those actions and dispositions – implied in individual or social life – to which their natural consequences bring their own penalties, there remains outside this sphere of emotion and struggle – and within a neutral zone in which a man simply exposes himself to man's curiosity – a certain rigidity of body, mind and character, that society would still like to get rid of in order to obtain from its members the greatest possible degree of elasticity and sociability. This rigidity is the comic, and laughter is its corrective.

Still, we must not accept this formula as a definition of the comic. It is suitable only for the cases that are elementary, theoretical and perfect, in which the comic is free from all adulteration. Nor do we offer it, either, as an explanation. We prefer to make it, if you will, the *leitmotiv* which is to accompany all our explanations. We must ever keep it in mind, though without dwelling on it too much, somewhat as a skilful fencer must think of the discontinuous movements of the lesson whilst his body is given up to the continuity of the fencing-match. We will now endeavour to reconstruct the sequence of comic forms, taking up again the thread that leads from the horse-play of a clown up to the most refined effects of comedy, following this thread in its often unforeseen windings, halting at intervals to look around, and finally getting back, if possible, to the point at

which the thread is dangling and where we shall perhaps find
– since the comic oscillates between life and art – the general
relation that art bears to life. ...

SOURCE: extract from *Le Rire* (1899); translated, by C. Brer-
eton and F. Rothwell, as *Laughter: An Essay on the Meaning of
the Comic* (London, 1911), pp. 18–22.

PART THREE

Twentieth-Century Views

1. THE TRADITIONS OF COMEDY

F. M. Cornford 'The Ritual Origins of Comedy' (1914)

... That Comedy sprang up and took shape in connection with Dionysiac or Phallic ritual has never been doubted. In the older histories of literature, it was customary to draw more or less imaginative pictures of village feasts in honour of the God of Wine, with processions and dances of wild disorder and drunken licence.[1] We were asked to conceive some rustic poet breaking out, when the new wine and the general excitement had gone to his head, into satirical sallies and buffooneries, taken up with shouts of laughter by the crowd of reeling revellers. The ultimate matter of Attic Comedy was to be sought in these songs and broad jokes, varied occasionally by a set match in abuse. ... We shall argue that Attic Comedy, as we know it from Aristophanes, is constructed in the framework of what was already a drama, a folk play; and that behind this folk play lay a still earlier phase, in which its action was dramatically presented in religious ritual. This view has the advantage of supposing that the element of dramatic representation was there from the very first. ...

SOME TYPES OF DRAMATIC FERTILITY RITUAL

Classification of Types
The forms taken by the rudimentary drama of the fertility ritual can be ranged under several heads. We shall here mention some of the most important, which specially concern us because we shall find clear traces of their influence on the comic plot. ...

All the varieties that we shall pass in review symbolise the same natural fact, which, in their primitive magical intention, they were designed to bring about and further by the familiar means of sympathetic or mimetic representation – the death of the old year and the birth or accession of the new, the decay and suspension of life in the frosts of winter and its release and *renouveau* in spring. Hence, in their essential core, they involve ... two aspects ... [of] phallic ritual: the expulsion of death, the induction of life. The ritual ceremonies may be classed according to the modes in which these two powers and the conflict between them [are] symbolised.

The Carrying Out of Death

In the simplest type, an effigy of the power of evil, often under the name of Death, is carried out and burnt, or thrown into the water, or otherwise destroyed. In ancient Greece a ceremony of this kind was held at Delphi, where a puppet called Charila was beaten by the King with his sandal, hanged, and buried in a precipitous chasm. The rite is identical in content, and not improbably even in name, with the Russian Funeral of Yarilo celebrated at the end of June. In this too, a puppet used to be put into a coffin, carried out of the town with dirges, and buried in the fields. Closely analogous to the Charila ceremony is the 'Driving Out of Hunger', recorded by Plutarch, at which a household slave was beaten with rods of a plant of cathartic powers and driven out of doors to the words, 'Out with hunger, in with wealth and health'.

This simple ritual formula reminds us that such ceremonies have commonly their other complementary half. If Hunger and Death are driven out, Wealth and Life must also be brought in to take their place. ...

The Greeks had their *Eiresione*, more than once mentioned by Aristophanes. ... The festival at which the *Eiresione* was carried about and hung up over the doors of houses was the early harvest festival of the Thargelia. This feast has links with the Dionysia that preceded it in the spring: both were under the management of the same magistrate, the Archon; both had cyclic choruses of men and boys. The Thargelia illustrates in distinct ceremonies each of the two aspects we have been considering – the induction of fruitfulness and wealth, and the expulsion of hunger, disease, sin, and death.

The bringing in of the new wealth of the harvest is symbolised in the simplest way by the procession of the *Eiresione*, an olive-branch, twined with wool, on which were hung figs and loaves, small vessels of wine and oil, and a drinking cup. It was carried by a boy who, in order to symbolise fulness of life and dissociation from any contact with death, was required to be ʼ$\alpha\mu\phi\iota\theta\alpha\lambda\dot{\eta}\varsigma$ [lit., 'blooming on both sides' –Ed.], the child of living parents. The other and darker side, the driving out of hunger, sin, and death, was expressed in the expulsion of the *Pharmakoi* [scapegoats –Ed.]. On the 6th of Thargelion [mid-May to mid-June –Ed.] two men, with strings of figs hung on them, black and white to show that one was for the men, the other for the women, were led out of the city and 'set in an appointed place'. There cheese, barley cakes and figs were put in their hands, and they were ceremonially beaten on the genital organs with leeks, branches of wild fig and other plants. Finally, it is said, they were burnt, and their ashes were scattered to the winds and into the sea, for a purification.

The point we wish to emphasise is that the *Pharmakos*, by some primitive conjunction difficult for us to grasp, is a representative both of the power of fertility and of the opposite powers of famine, disease, impurity, death. The ceremonies of the *Pharmakos* and the *Eiresione* are complementary. At the former we have the human victim, at the latter an olive-branch, conducted in procession. Both are hung with fruits. The *Eiresione*, again, has its figs, loaves, and vessels of wine and oil; the *Pharmakos* is given figs, a barley-cake, and cheese. Each has even its drinking-cup; for a *kylix* was hung on the *Eiresione*, 'that it might go drunk to bed'; while the *Pharmakos* carried a *phiale*, the ritual theft of which from the temple of Apollo was yearly enacted as part of the ceremony. The human victims, with their burden of sin and death, are driven out and consumed with fire. Their ashes are scattered, both to get rid of the evil and to distribute the good fertility charm over the fields. They cannot be brought back again. In their place, the *Eiresione* branch comes in, bearing the wealth of the year and the promise of life and food in abundance. Our authorities do not tell us when this second ceremony occurred; but it is a natural conjecture that it was connected with the procession on the second and happy day of the festival, Thargelion 7.

We may take note here that one play of Aristophanes, the *Plutus*, is on the theme: 'Out with Poverty and Hunger, in with Wealth and Health'. Wealth is brought into the house, which overflows with abundance; Poverty, who comes to make her protest and plead her beneficence in the *Agon*, is driven away with curses, like a *Pharmakos*.

The Fight of Summer and Winter

In other cases, the two powers of evil and good are personified as two antagonists who fight together. This clear distinction and opposition of the two spirits is easy, because, in the succession of the seasons, each in turn has his separate reigns, the period during which he triumphs over his rival. 'Thus in the towns of Sweden on May Day two troops of young men on horseback used to meet as if for mortal combat. One of them was led by a representative of Winter clad in furs, who threw snowballs and ice in order to prolong the cold weather. The other troop was commanded by a representative of Summer covered with fresh leaves and flowers. In the sham fight which followed the party of Summer came off victorious, and the ceremony ended with a feast.' [2]

Usener explained on these lines the Macedonian *Xandika*, held in the month Xandikos before the Spring equinox. The rite marked the opening of the campaigning season, and was regarded as a purification of the army. On the occasion described by Livy it consisted of three parts. First came the *Lustration:* the army marched between the two halves of a slain dog. Then followed the Parade (*Decursus*); and finally the two halves of the army engaged in a sham fight, led by the two royal princes. A banquet and *Kómos* [festival procession –Ed.] followed in the evening. [3]

The combat often takes forms which are still familiar as games. The Tug-of-War, for instance, is practised among many primitive peoples as a magical means of procuring the victory of the powers of fertility. A well-known case is the autumn contest among the Central Esquimaux, in which two parties –

the Ptarmigans comprising all persons born in winter and the
Ducks all persons born in summer – tug at a long rope of
sealskin. If the Ptarmigans are beaten, then Summer has won
the game and fine weather may be expected in the coming
winter. In his general remarks on ceremonies of this type, Dr
Frazer says: 'We may surmise that in many cases the two con-
tending parties represent respectively the powers of good and
evil struggling against each other, for the mastery.'[4]

The Young and the Old King

In the battle of Summer and Winter the two powers are clearly
opposed and distinct. In other forms the good spirit and his
antagonist are felt to be, after all, only two successive representatives of the same principle. Here again, the explanation is
obvious with reference to the order of time. The spirit of the new
year and of its fertility is merely the spirit of the old year come
back again. The old year is a force of evil and obstruction, only
because it has grown old and yielded to the decay of winter.
When this is remembered, the contest may take the form of a
struggle between the Old and the Young King, ending in the
death of the former and the succession of the latter to his throne.
[We may cite] the myth of Pelops, who defeats the old
weather-king, Oenomaus, and wins his daughter, Hippodamia.
Oedipus, again, kills his father Laius, marries the Queen, and
succeeds to the kingdom. There are many other similar stories
of the contest for the hand of a princess which carries the
kingdom with it. In this type, it must be noted, the action ends
in the triumph of the new King and the sacred marriage with
the local Earth Goddess. Another widespread version makes the
hero rescue his bride from a monster. St George defeats the
dragon and carries off Sabra, the king of Egypt's daughter;
Perseus rescues Andromeda; Heracles delivers Hesione, and so
on. Besides the monster, the hero in these stories often has to
deal with two other forms of the antagonist – the wicked Old
King (a Laomedon or an Eurystheus), who would defraud
him of his rightful reward, and an imposter who falsely pretends
to have killed the monster and all but wins the bride, when the
hero appears in the nick of time with convincing proof of his
own claim.

The Death and Resurrection Type

Another very important variant is that in which the same Spirit of Life dies yearly and is brought back to life. In this form the identity of the old Year Spirit with the new is recognised still more clearly than in the contest of the old and the new king. We cannot here discuss the implications and developments of this rite, which may, in its origin, be linked with the mock death and resurrection of the candidates for tribal initiation, and undoubtedly gives rise to a certain type of mystical 'sacrifice'. But a few points must here be noted. The first is that in this form it is the good principle that is slain; its triumph, the necessary conclusion to a ritual designed for a beneficial purpose, must take the form of a resurrection. Again, the killing may be done either by the worshippers themselves, who tear the representative of the spirit to pieces (σπαραγμός) and then lament his death, or by a wicked antagonist, in which case the death will be preceded by a contest similar to those we have passed in review. . . .

Such are some of the chief varieties of the dramatic ritual associated with the renewal of life in spring. The essential content of them all is ultimately the same as that of the Phallic Song, the victory of the Spirit of Life over the adverse influences of blight and death. The only difference is that this Spirit, instead of being merely invoked to be present at the procession of his worshippers, is visibly embodied in the person of one of them, and his contest with the adversary, his death and resurrection, are enacted in the pantomime. . . .

SOURCE: extracts from *The Origin of Attic Comedy* (London, 1914), pp. 3–4, 53–60.

NOTES

[Abbreviated and reorganised from the original –Ed.]

1. [Ed.] On this, see discussion of the etymological derivation of Comedy in the Introduction, above.

2. Sir James George Frazer, *The Golden Bough: A Study in Comparative Religion*, 1st edn, in 2 vols (London, 1890); 12th edn, in 12 vols (1915); one-

vol. abridgement (1922), with paperback version (1957, and reprints): ch. xxviii, § 5, p. 416.

3. [Ed.] See discussion of *Kómos* in Introduction, above.

4. Frazer, op. cit.

Northrop Frye   The Argument of Comedy   (1949)

The Greeks produced two kinds of comedy, Old Comedy, represented by the eleven extant plays of Aristophanes, and New
Comedy, of which the best known exponent is Menander.
About two dozen New Comedies survive in the work of [the
Roman playwrights] Plautus and Terence. Old Comedy, however, was out of date before Aristophanes himself was dead; and
today, when we speak of comedy, we normally think of something that derives from the Menander tradition.

New Comedy unfolds from what may be described as a comic
Oedipus situation. Its main theme is the successful effort of a
young man to outwit an opponent and possess the girl of his
choice. The opponent is usually the father (*senex*), and the
psychological descent of the heroine from the mother is also
sometimes hinted at. The father frequently wants the same girl,
and is cheated out of her by the son, the mother thus becoming
the son's ally. The girl is usually a slave or courtesan, and the
plot turns on a *cognitio* or discovery of birth which makes her
marriageable. Thus it turns out that she is not under an insu-
perable taboo after all but is an accessible object of desire, so
that the plot follows the regular wish-fulfilment pattern. Often
the central Oedipus situation is thinly concealed by surrogates
or doubles of the main characters, as when the heroine is dis-
covered to be the hero's sister, and has to be married off to his
best friend. In Congreve's *Love for Love*, to take a modern instance well within the Menandrine tradition, there are two
Oedipus themes in counterpoint: the hero cheats his father out
of the heroine, and the best friend violates the wife of an impotent old man who is the heroine's guardian. Whether this
analysis is sound or not, New Comedy is certainly concerned
with the manoeuvring of a young man toward a young woman,
and marriage is the tonic chord on which it ends. The normal
comic resolution is the surrender of the *senex* to the hero, never
the reverse. Shakespeare tried to reverse the pattern in *All's*

Well That Ends Well, where the king of France forces Bertram to marry Helena, and the critics have not yet stopped making faces over it.

New Comedy has the blessing of Aristotle, who greatly preferred it to its predecessor, and it exhibits the general pattern of Aristotelian causation. It has a material cause in the young man's sexual desire, and a formal cause in the social order represented by the *senex,* with which the hero comes to terms when he gratifies his desire. It has an efficient cause in the character who brings about the final situation. In classical times this character is a tricky slave; Renaissance dramatists often use some adaptation of the medieval 'vice'; modern writers generally like to pretend that nature, or at least the natural course of events, is the efficient cause. The final cause is the audience, which is expected by its applause to take part in the comic resolution. All this takes place on a single order of existence. The action of New Comedy tends to become probable rather than fantastic, and it moves toward realism and away from myth and romance. The one romantic (originally mythical) feature in it, the fact that the hero or heroine turns out to be freeborn or someone's heir, is precisely the feature that trained New Comedy audiences tire of most quickly.

The conventions of New Comedy are the conventions of Jonson and Molière, and *a fortiori* of the English Restoration and the French rococo. When Ibsen started giving ironic twists to the same formulas, his startled hearers took them for portents of a social revolution. Even the old chestnut about the heroine's being really the hero's sister turns up in *Ghosts* and *Little Eyolf.* The average movie of today is a rigidly conventionalised New Comedy proceeding toward an act which, like death in Greek Tragedy, takes place offstage, and is symbolised by the final embrace.

In all good New Comedy there is a social as well as an individual theme which must be sought in the general atmosphere of reconcilation that makes the final marriage possible. As the hero gets closer to the heroine and opposition is overcome, all the right-thinking people come over to his side. Thus a new social unit is formed on the stage, and the moment that this social unit crystallises is the moment of the comic resolution.

In the last scene, when the dramatist usually tries to get all his characters on the stage at once, the audience witnesses the birth of a renewed sense of social integration. In comedy as in life the regular expression of this is a festival, whether a marriage, a dance or a feast. Old Comedy has, besides a marriage, a *komos*, the processional dance from which comedy derives its name; and the masque, which is a by-form of comedy, also ends in a dance.

This new social integration may be called, first, a kind of moral norm and, second, the pattern of a free society. We can see this more clearly if we look at the sort of characters who impede the progress of the comedy toward the hero's victory. These are always people who are in some kind of mental bondage, who are helplessly driven by ruling passions, neurotic compulsions, social rituals and selfishness. The miser, the hypochondriac, the hypocrite, the pedant, the snob: these are humors, people who do not fully know what they are doing, who are slaves to a predictable self-imposed pattern of behavior. What we call the moral norm is, then, not morality but deliverance from moral bondage. Comedy is designed not to condemn evil, but to ridicule a lack of self-knowledge. It finds the virtues of Malvolio and Angelo as comic as the vices of Shylock.

The essential comic resolution, therefore, is an individual release which is also a social reconciliation. The normal individual is freed from the bonds of a humorous society, and a normal society is freed from the bonds imposed on it by humorous individuals. The Oedipus pattern we noted in New Comedy belongs to the individual side of this, and the sense of the ridiculousness of the humor to the social side. But all real comedy is based on the principle that these two forms of release are ultimately the same: this principle may be seen at its most concentrated in *The Tempest*. The rule holds whether the resolution is expressed in social terms, as in *The Merchant of Venice*, or in individual terms, as in Ibsen's *An Enemy of the People*.

The freer the society, the greater the variety of individuals it can tolerate, and the natural tendency of comedy is to include as many as possible in its final festival. The motto of comedy is Terence's 'Nothing human is alien to me'. This may be one reason for the traditional comic importance of the parasite, who has no business to be at the festival but is nevertheless there. The spirit of reconciliation which pervades the comedies of Shakespeare is not to be ascribed to a personal attitude of his own, about which we know nothing whatever, but to his impersonal concentration of the laws of comic form.

Hence the moral quality of the society presented is not the point of the comic resolution. In Jonson's *Volpone* the final assertion of the moral norm takes the form of a social revenge on Volpone, and the play ends with a great bustle of sentences to penal servitude and the galleys. One feels perhaps that the audience's sense of the moral norm does not need so much hard labor. In *The Alchemist*, when Love-wit returns to his house, the virtuous characters have proved so weak and the rascals so ingenious that the action dissolves in laughter. Whichever is morally the better ending, that of *The Alchemist* is more concentrated comedy. *Volpone* is starting to move toward tragedy, toward the vision of a greatness which develops *hybris* and catastrophe.

The same principle is even clearer in Aristophanes. Aristophanes is the most personal of writers: his opinions on every subject are written all over his plays, and we have no doubt of his moral attitude. We know that he wanted peace with Sparta and that he hated Cleon, and when his comedy depicts the attaining of peace and the defeat of Cleon we know that he approved and wanted his audience to approve. But in *Ecclesiazusae* a band of women in disguise railroad a communistic scheme through the Assembly, which is a horrid parody of Plato's *Republic*, and proceed to inaugurate Plato's sexual communism with some astonishing improvements. Presumably Aristophanes did not applaud this, yet the comedy follows the same pattern and the same resolution. In *The Birds* the Peisthetairos who defies Zeus and blocks out Olympus with his Cloud-Cuckoo-Land is accorded the same triumph that is given to the Trygaeus of the *Peace* who flies to heaven and brings a golden age back to Athens.

Comedy, then, may show virtue her own feature and scorn her own image – for Hamlet's famous definition of drama was originally a definition of comedy. It may emphasise the birth of an ideal society as you like it, or the tawdriness of the sham society which is the way of the world. There is an important parallel here with tragedy. Tragedy, we are told, is expected to raise, but not ultimately to accept, the emotions of pity and terror. These I take to be the sense of moral good and evil, respectively, which we attach to the tragic hero. He may be as good as Caesar, and so appeal to our pity, or as bad as Macbeth, and so appeal to terror, but the particular thing called tragedy that happens to him does not depend on moral status. The tragic catharsis passes beyond moral judgment, and while it is quite possible to construct a moral tragedy, what tragedy gains in morality it loses in cathartic power. The same is true of the comic catharsis, which raises sympathy and ridicule on a moral basis, but passes beyond both.

Many things are involved in the tragic catharsis, but one of them is a mental or imaginative form of the sacrificial ritual out of which tragedy arose. This is the ritual of the struggle, death and rebirth of a God-Man, which is linked to the yearly triumph of spring over winter. The tragic hero is not really killed, and the audience no longer eats his body and drinks his blood, but the corresponding thing in art still takes place. The audience enters into communion with the body of the hero, becoming thereby a single body itself. Comedy grows out of the same ritual, for in the ritual the tragic story has a comic sequel. Divine men do not die: they die and rise again. The ritual pattern behind the catharsis of comedy is the resurrection that follows the death, the epiphany or manifestation of the risen hero. This is clear enough in Aristophanes, where the hero is treated as a risen God-Man, led in triumph with the divine honors of the Olympic victor, rejuvenated or hailed as a new Zeus. In New Comedy the new human body is, as we have seen, both a hero and a social group. Aristophanes is not only closer to the ritual pattern, but contemporary with Plato; and his comedy, unlike Menander's, is Platonic and dialectic: it seeks not the entelechy of the soul but the Form of the Good, and finds it in the resurrection of the soul from the world of the cave to the sunlight. The audience gains a vision of that resurrection whether the conclusion is joyful or ironic, just as in tragedy it gains a vision of a heroic death whether the hero is morally innocent or guilty.

Two things follow from this: first, that tragedy is really implicit or uncompleted comedy; second, that comedy contains a potential tragedy within itself. With regard to the latter, Aristophanes is full of traces of the original death of the hero which preceded his resurrection in the ritual. Even in New Comedy the dramatist usually tries to bring his action as close to a tragic overthrow of the hero as he can get it, and reverses this movement as suddenly as possible. In Plautus the tricky slave is often forgiven or even freed after having been threatened with all the brutalities that a very brutal dramatist can think of, including crucifixion. Thus the resolution of New Comedy seems to be a realistic foreshortening of a death-and-resurrection pattern, in which the struggle and rebirth of a divine hero has shrunk into a marriage, the freeing of a slave, and the triumph of a young man over an older one.

As for the conception of tragedy as implicit comedy, we may notice how often tragedy closes on the major chord of comedy: the Aeschylean trilogy, for instance, proceeds to what is really a comic resolution, and so do many tragedies of Euripides. From the point of view of Christianity, too, tragedy is an episode in that larger scheme of redemption and resurrection to which Dante gave the name of *commedia*. This conception of *commedia* enters drama with the miracle-play cycles, where such tragedies as the Fall and the Crucifixion are episodes of a dramatic scheme in which the divine comedy has the last word. The sense of tragedy as a prelude to comedy is hardly separable from anything explicitly Christian. The serenity of the final double chorus in the St Matthew Passion would hardly be attainable if composer and audience did not know that there was more to the story. Nor would the death of Samson lead to 'calm of mind all passion spent' if Samson were not a prototype of the rising Christ.

New Comedy is thus contained, so to speak, within the symbolic structure of Old Comedy, which in its turn is contained within the Christian conception of *commedia*. This sounds like a logically exhaustive classification, but we have still not caught Shakespeare in it.

It is only in Jonson and the Restoration writers that English comedy can be called a form of New Comedy. The earlier tradition established by Peele and developed by Lyly, Greene and the masque writers, which uses themes from romance and folklore and avoids the comedy of manners, is the one followed by Shakespeare. These themes are largely medieval in origin, and derive, not from the mysteries or the moralities or the interludes, but from a fourth dramatic tradition. This is the drama of folk ritual, of the St George play and the mummer's play, of the feast of the ass and the Boy Bishop, and of all the dramatic activity that punctuated the Christian calendar with the rituals of an immemorial paganism. We may call this the drama of the green world, and its theme is once again the triumph of life over the waste land, the death and revival of the year impersonated by figures still human, and once divine as well.

When Shakespeare began to study Plautus and Terence, his dramatic instinct, stimulated by his predecessors, divined that there was a profounder pattern in the argument of comedy than appears in either of them. At once – for the process is beginning in *The Comedy of Errors* – he started groping toward that profounder pattern, the ritual of death and revival that also underlies Aristophanes, of which an exact equivalent lay ready to hand in the drama of the green world. This parallelism largely accounts for the resemblances to Greek ritual which Colin Still has pointed out in *The Tempest*.

The Two Gentlemen of Verona is an orthodox New Comedy except for one thing. The hero Valentine becomes captain of a band of outlaws in a forest, and all the other characters are gathered into this forest and become converted. Thus the action of the comedy begins in a world represented as a normal world, moves into the green world, goes into a metamorphosis there in which the comic resolution is achieved, and returns to the normal world. The forest in this play is the embryonic form of the fairy world of *A Midsummer Night's Dream*, the Forest of Arden in *As You Like It*, Windsor Forest in *The Merry Wives of Windsor*, and the pastoral world of the mythical sea-coasted Bohemia in *The Winter's Tale*. In all these comedies there is the same rhythmic movement from normal world to green world and back again. Nor is this second world confined to the forest comedies. In *The Merchant of Venice* the two worlds are a little harder to see, yet Venice is clearly not the same world as that of

Portia's mysterious house in Belmont, where there are caskets teaching that gold and silver are corruptible goods, and from whence proceed the wonderful cosmological harmonies of the fifth act. In *The Tempest* the entire action takes place in the second world, and the same may be said of *Twelfth Night*, which, as its title implies, presents a carnival society: not so much a green world as an evergreen one. The second world is absent from the so-called problem comedies, which is one of the things that makes them problem comedies.

The green world charges the comedies with a symbolism in which the comic resolution contains a suggestion of the old ritual pattern of the victory of summer over winter. This is explicit in *Love's Labour's Lost*. In this very masque-like play, the comic contest takes the form of the medieval debate of winter and spring. In *The Merry Wives of Windsor* there is an elaborate ritual of the defeat of winter, known to folklorists as 'carrying out Death', of which Falstaff is the victim; and Falstaff must have felt that, after being thrown into the water, dressed up as a witch and beaten out of the house with curses, and finally supplied with a beast's head and singed with candles while he said, 'Divide me like a brib'd buck, each a haunch', he had done about all that could reasonably be asked of any fertility spirit.

The association of this symbolism with the death and revival of human beings is more elusive, but still perceptible. The fact that the heroine often brings about the comic resolution by disguising herself as a boy is familiar enough. In the Hero of *Much Ado About Nothing* and the Helena of *All's Well That Ends Well*, this theme of the withdrawal and return of the heroine comes as close to a death and revival as Elizabethan conventions will allow. The Thaisa of *Pericles* and the Fidele of *Cymbeline* are beginning to crack the conventions, and with the disappearance and revival of Hermione in *The Winter's Tale*, who actually returns once as a ghost in a dream, the original nature-myth of Demeter and Proserpine is openly established. The fact that the dying and reviving character is usually female strengthens the feeling that there is something maternal about the green world, in which the new order of the comic resolution is nourished and brought to birth. However, a similar theme which is very like the rejuvenation of the *senex* so frequent in Aristophanes occurs in the folklore motif of the healing of the impotent king on which *All's Well That Ends Well* is based, and this theme is probably involved in the symbolism of Prospero.

The conception of a second world bursts the boundaries of Menandrine comedy, yet it is clear that the world of Puck is no world of eternal forms or divine revelation. Shakespeare's comedy is not Aristotelian and realistic like Menander's, nor Platonic and dialectic like Aristophanes', nor Thomist and sacramental like Dante's, but a fourth kind. It is an Elizabethan kind, and is not confined either to Shakespeare or to the drama. Spenser's epic is a wonderful contrapuntal intermingling of two orders of existence: one the red and white world of English history, the other the green world of the Faerie Queene. The latter is a world of crusading virtues proceeding from the Faerie Queene's court and designed to return to that court when the destiny of the other world is fulfilled. The fact that the Faerie Queene's knights are sent out during the twelve days of the Christmas festival suggests our next point.

Shakespeare, too, has his green world of comedy and his red and white world of history. The story of the latter is at one point interrupted by an invasion from the comic world, when Falstaff *senex et parasitus* throws his gigantic shadow over Prince Henry, assuming on one occasion the role of his father. Clearly, if the Prince is ever to conquer France he must reassert the moral norm. The moral norm is duly reasserted, but the rejection of Falstaff is not a comic resolution. In comedy the moral norm is not morality but deliverance, and we certainly do not feel delivered from Falstaff as we feel delivered from Shylock with his absurd and vicious bond. The moral norm does not carry with it the vision of a free society: Falstaff will always keep a bit of that in his tavern.

Falstaff is a mock king, a lord of misrule, and his tavern is a Saturnalia. Yet we are reminded of the original meaning of the Saturnalia, as a rite intended to recall the golden age of Saturn. Falstaff's world is not a golden world, but as long as we remember it we cannot forget that the world of *Henry IV* is an iron one. We are reminded too of another traditional denizen of the green world, Robin Hood, the outlaw who manages to suggest a better kind of society than those who make him an outlaw can produce. The outlaws in *The Two Gentlemen of Verona* compare themselves, in spite of the Italian setting, to Robin Hood; and in *As You Like It* Charles the wrestler says of Duke Senior's followers: 'There they live like the old Robin Hood of England; they say many young gentlemen flock to him every day, and fleet the time carelessly, as they did in the golden world.'

In the histories, therefore, the comic Saturnalia is a temporary reversal of normal standards: comic 'relief' as it is called, which subsides and allows the history to continue. In the comedies, the green world suggests an original golden age which the normal world has usurped and which makes us wonder if it is not the normal world that is the real Saturnalia. In *Cymbeline* the green world finally triumphs over a historical theme, the reason being perhaps that in that play the incarnation of Christ, which is contemporary with Cymbeline, takes place offstage, and accounts for the halcyon peace with which the play concludes. From then on in Shakespeare's plays, the green world has it all its own way, and both in *Cymbeline* and in *Henry VIII* there may be suggestions that Shakespeare, like Spenser, is moving toward a synthesis of the two worlds; a wedding of Prince Arthur and the Faerie Queene.

This world of fairies, dreams, disembodied souls and pastoral lovers may not be a 'real' world, but, if not, there is something equally illusory in the stumbling and blinded follies of the 'normal' world, of Theseus's Athens with its idiotic marriage law, of Duke Frederick and his melancholy tyranny, of Leontes and his mad jealousy, of the Court Party with their plots and intrigues. The famous speech of Prospero about the dream nature of reality applies equally to Milan and the enchanted island. We spend our lives partly in a waking world we call normal and partly in a dream world which we create out of our own desires. Shakespeare endows both worlds with equal imaginative power, brings them opposite one another, and makes each world seem unreal when seen by the light of the other. He uses freely both the heroic triumph of New Comedy and the ritual resurrection of its predecessor, but his distinctive comic resolution is different from either: it is a detachment of the spirit born of this reciprocal reflection of two illusory realities. We need not ask whether this brings us into a higher order of existence or not, for the question of existence is not relevant to poetry.

We have spoken of New Comedy as Aristotelian, Old Comedy as Platonic and Dante's *commedia* as Thomist; but it is difficult to suggest a philosophical spokesman for the form of Shakespeare's comedy. For Shakespeare, the subject matter of poetry is not life, or nature, or reality, or relevation, or anything else that the philosopher builds on, but poetry itself, a verbal universe. That is one reason why he is both the most elusive and the most substantial of poets.

SOURCE: essay on 'The Argument of Comedy', in *English Institute Essays, 1948* (New York, 1949), pp. 58–73.

Walter Kaiser   'The Wisdom of the Fool'   (1963)

... It was the Renaissance that brought the fool into the lime-light on the stage of literature; and though he has antecedents as far back as the world of classical antiquity, the figure evoked by the word *fool* is really a creation of the late Middle Ages. When we hear the word, we think of a small, dwarfish man, often hunchbacked, who wears a coat of motley with its asinine hood and bells, and carries a bauble or marotte. Of course, there is also a less specific connotation to the word *fool*: prover-bially, it refers simply to any human being who is deprived of reason – the stupid, the ignorant, the mad, the fool-ish. The Rigoletto-type fool evoked by the word – the court jester of the fifteenth century – is in fact only the formal, artificial imitation of the actual fools, the madmen and idiots, who wandered loose through the medieval world. Between the two extremes of the village idiot and the court jester, the natural and the artificial fool, there are as many degrees of fooldom and foolery as there are degrees of madness; but whoever is called foolish, whether the lover, the dupe, the sinner or the theatrical clown, is called so because he acts like a man deprived of his wits – like the natural fool. Upon this 'bell without a clapper', as he was sometimes called, the Middle Ages rang many changes, and when the first major fool of the Renaissance exclaims, 'Good lorde, what a *Theatre* is this worlde? how many, and divers are the pageants that fooles plaie therein?',[1] she calls to mind all of the many fools that the Middle Ages had developed.

These types and their social, literary and theatrical histories have been carefully traced and catalogued, notably by Olive Busby, Barbara Swain, and Enid Welsford, and their studies are an essential introduction to any examination of the Renais-sance fool. To reiterate all that has been written on this would require a lengthy digression from our subject, and there is little need to repeat what has been so adequately set forth elsewhere. It may be useful, however, to summarise briefly what the

Middle Ages thought a fool was, especially since the Renaissance authors whom we shall be considering assumed that their readers had a certain image of the fool in mind.

Since it is upon the prototype of the natural fool that all the more sophisticated and artificial fools are based, we may see these attitudes most clearly and in their most pristine form if we consider what the Middle Ages thought of the simple idiot. The first point to be made is that they knew him well. Indeed, it is hard for us to imagine how common the spectacle of idiocy or insanity must have been in a world that knew neither the techniques of modern medicine nor those of the psychological clinic. Generally such creatures could be seen almost everywhere. Violent madmen, of course, who were thought to be possessed by devils, were tortured and incarcerated, first in the monasteries and later in such institutions as that celebrated etymological source, the Hospital of St Mary of Bethlehem in London. On the other hand, the feeble-minded were simply allowed to roam free, for they were harmless. Their heads seemed as empty as a pair of bellows, and accordingly from the Latin word for bellows the name *fool* or *fou* was coined for them. Set apart from normal human beings by his empty-headed irrationality, the innocent fool was to the Middle Ages more of a thing than a being, and he became to them simply an object of fun or pity or veneration. For the stupidity of his words and deeds he was often derided; for his inability to behave and understand like other people he was sometimes pitied; and occasionally, because he was thought to be under the special protection of God, he was venerated. For all three reasons he was tolerated.

That such a fool was called 'natural' is particularly significant and was to have, especially in the sixteenth century, vast implications. He was, of course, seen as a natural fool because he was thought to have been created foolish by nature. Yet the fact that such an adjective was considered necessary implies that artificial fools, from whom natural fools had to be distinguished, had come into existence. Accordingly, it is not until the fifteenth century, after dramatic and court fools have been developed, that the adjective 'natural' is applied in this connection. Later, in the sixteenth century, the phrase had become sufficiently common to be abbreviated; and it is, appropriately enough, from the pen of Sir Thomas More (whose name in Greek means 'fool', who kept a famous fool as a member of his household, and whom Erasmus considered the fool *par excellence*) that we have the first recorded reference to a natural fool as simply 'a natural'. But the adjective is fitting for the fool in other ways as well. As the child of nature, for example, his appetites and desires are wholly natural. The idiot performs his natural functions naturally, without sophistication or the usage of custom: when he is sad, he cries; when he is happy, he laughs; when he is hungry, he eats. Unconscious of the rules of propriety, he says and does whatever is natural for him to say or do at any given moment. He lives in the fullness of that moment, for he is not intelligent enough to remember the past or to anticipate the future; though he may be frightened by palpable physical threats, the cares and fears of the intellect are obviously unknown to him. For this reason, he was often deemed happier in his simplicity than other men in their wisdom, and Robert Burton was simply expanding into a sophisticated scepticism an attitude that had been prevalent for centuries when he wrote:

Some think fools and disards live the merriest lives, as Ajax in Sophocles; *nihil scire vita jucundissima*; 'tis the pleasantest life to know nothing; *iners malorum remedium ignorantia*; ignorance is a down-right remedy of evils. These curious and laborious sciences, Galens, Tullies, Aristotles, Justinians, do but trouble the world, some think; we might live better with that illiterate Virginian simplicity, and gross ignorance; entire ideots do best; they are not macerated with cares, tormented with fear and anxieties as other men are: for, as he said, if folly were a pain, you should hear them houl, roar and cry out in every house, as you go by in the street; but they are most free, jocund, and merry, and, in some countries, as amongst the Turks, honoured for saints, and abundantly maintained out of the common stock.[2]

Since he does not comprehend the conventions of society, the natural fool is invariably irreverent of those conventions, not out of any motives of iconoclasm but simply because he does not know any better. This fact, of course, poses a problem for society, because the fool is a potentially subversive element in its midst. For the most part, however, the Middle Ages tended to tolerate the fool's nonconformity; and, though he might appear to mock the laws of society and religion, men tended to understand that the mockery was not intentional, that the natural was simply being his natural self. He was therefore not expected to obey any code, and in this respect medieval tolerance gave the idiot considerable freedom to speak and act in ways for which others would have been summarily punished. To be sure, there were often severe Gonerils who found the fool's behavior too trying to be borne; but for the most part he was 'all-licensed', and a comparatively complete freedom was always associated with the natural fool. What he said was either an hilarious joke or, at the very worst, a foolish impertinence which merited him little more than a box on the ears or bed without supper. He was treated, in short, like a child because he had only the intelligence of a child.

It is not hard to see how the combination of the humor he provided and the impunity he enjoyed made him irresistible to the literary imagination. His beguiling, childlike appeal guaranteed him the sympathy of the audience, and at the same time his traditional freedom from punishment made it possible for the author to have him speak out boldly. If anyone should object to what the fool said, it was easy to point out that it was, after all, only a fool who said it. Thus the licence of the natural fool was appropriated for the artificial fool; his nonconformity was turned into iconoclasm, his naturalism into anarchy, and his frankness into satire. Whether in the court or on the stage, he was able to criticise the accepted order of things and to voice daring indictments of the church or the throne or the law or society in general. When a normal, reasonable man's natural desires urge him to rebel against some such order, he is expected to 'know better'. But because the fool is not expected to *know* anything, he readily became an expression of all the mischievous and rebellious desires in man which society attempts to control or frustrate. In the eternal polemic between law and nature, the head and the heart, the artificially imitated natural fool, whose head was only an empty bellows, was brought forth as the champion of the lawless heart. He was a difficult adversary to combat, precisely because he was only a fool.

If the medieval idiot was countenanced by the society toward which he was subversive, he was also countenanced by the religion of which he was irreverent; and it is from the theological justifications of the fool that the profoundest aspects of his symbolic role were developed. As I have already noted, the feeble-minded were considered by the Middle Ages to be under the special protection of God, and they were tolerated (if not always envied) for this reason above all else. Christ himself had, of course, given the example by favoring fools and idiots and children and by exalting, in such utterances as the Sermon on the Mount, the simple in heart. In the fool God had seemed to create those simple idiots of whom Christ had spoken, and the fool's affinities to the natural order often appeared to indicate a special affinity with God. This seemed especially so of the fool's speech which, for all its ignorance, at times managed to pierce through the veils of convention and propriety to the profound simplicity of a Christlike truth. At such times it was assumed that God had entered into the fool and spoken through his mouth, and this was perhaps the most important reason for granting fools great freedom of speech; it was always possible that when the fool's babbling was not idiotic it was theopneustic ['God-inspired' –Ed.]. Theologically, such an attitude toward the fool was authorised by St Paul, who often explained (especially in his epistles to the Corinthians) that men must become fools for Christ's sake, and commanded that those who are considered wise by the world should become fools in order that they may be truly wise. Such Pauline paradoxes were received with particular favor, as one might expect, by the medieval mystics; and all through the Middle Ages the tradition of the Fool in Christ, whether articulated precisely as such or not, was preserved by such figures as Gregory the Great, Scotus Erigena, Francis of Assisi, Jacopone da Todi and Raimond Lull.

It was quite late in the Middle Ages, however, and from that northern mysticism which we associate with the names of Eckhart, Tauler, Ruysbroek and Groot, and the movement known as the *devotio moderna*, that the humble, analphabetic fool received his most articulate theological justification. Two men in particular, Thomas à Kempis and Nicholas of Cusa, gave the medieval world its final theological apologies for the fool: the one in his manual, *Imitatio Christi*, and the other in his treatise,

De docta ignorantia. Coincidentally, Kempis finished the last of many versions of his book in 1441, and Cusanus's book first appeared in 1440. It is more than coincidence, however, that in their youth they both attended that school at Deventer which Erasmus was later to attend: the 'holy simplicity' of Kempis, the 'learned ignorance' of Cusanus and the 'wise fool' of Erasmus are all ideologically derived (at least in part) from the Philosophy of Christ taught at Deventer. This philosophy, in opposing the prevalent scholastic learning, exalted a simple Christianity and a way of life that imitated the foolishness of Christ. Accordingly, Kempis's book prescribed for a man a life which, in its pietistic simplicity and humility, resembled that of the fool, and Cusanus in his works laid the philosophical foundations for the concept of the wisdom of folly.

Of the two men, Kempis had the greater practical influence upon later generations, and his book was the more widely read. Cusanus's cryptic, elusive, paradoxical expositions of his philosophy have never achieved the same popularity, and it is only recently that they have even been properly evaluated. But in the history of the figure of the fool (not to mention that of the philosophy of knowledge), Cusanus's work is by far the more important; for, with its fusion of Pauline theology and the Neoplatonism of the pseudo-Dionysius, it established a philosophical schema out of which the first of the great sixteenth-century fools was created. In the two paradoxical keystones of Cusanus's philosophy, *docta ignorantia* and *coincidentia oppositorum*, both the philosophical and stylistic characteristics of Erasmus's Stultitia find their first extensive exposition. The questions that Cusanus poses about the possibility of knowledge, the wisdom he derives from the antithesis between the irrational absolute and logical reason, and the rejection of rational theology to which these lead him, help to form the philosophical assumptions upon which Erasmus's concept of the fool is based. Similarly, that irony which, as we shall see, is the essential mode of expression for Erasmus's fool is the result of what Cusanus called the 'coincidentia scientiae et ignorantiae, seu doctae ignorantiae'. That ability of reason to question itself and yet emerge with wisdom, which Erwin Panofsky has seen as a characteristic of Renaissance thought and which he finds per-

fectly exemplified in Erasmus's *Moriae encomium*,[3] is the infor-
mative characteristic of all Cusanus's antithetical, paradoxical
philosophy; and Ernst Cassirer has claimed that 'every study
that is directed towards comprehending the philosophy of the
Renaissance as a systematic unity must take as its point of
departure the doctrine of Nicholas Cusanus.'[4]

'Everything is folly in this world', commented Leopardi one
December day in 1823 in his encyclopedic *Zibaldone*, 'except to
play the fool.' His formulation may be said to describe the point
at which the concept of the fool had arrived by the end of the
fifteenth century. Most of the world seemed to be made up of
fools, as Brandt showed in 1494 in the passenger list of his
Narrenschiff. The exception, as Cusanus had philosophised and
as Erasmus was to demonstrate in fifteen years, was the fool
himself; and this paradox was, by the end of the century, contained within the very word *fool*. For while, on the one hand, it
remained a term of opprobrium or condescension (with a mer-
cilessly enlarged application), on the other hand, it had become
a term of praise and aspiration. One could say of an idiot that
he was only a fool because he was not wise; but one could also
say of a wise man that he would be wiser if he were a fool. Such
universality gave the fool a predominance that enabled him
symbolically to dominate a major aspect of the thought of the
following century when, after playing a minor role on the stage
throughout the late Middle Ages, he steps forward at the height
of the Renaissance to assume one of the main roles in life's
drama. As he enacts the part of the protagonist down the length
of the sixteenth century, he gives articulation to the doubts and
uncertainties of one of the great ideological upheavals in human
history; 'for the development of the idea of the fool', as Enid
Welsford has said, 'is one of the products of that uneasy time of
transition when the great medieval synthesis was shattered and
the new order (if order it was) had not yet been established'.[5]
As the sober figures of the monk, the pilgrim, the knight and
the scholar begin their long exits, the irreverent, irrational,
laughing figure of the fool comes capering forward to take over
the play. 'Across Europe', in Harry Levin's description, 'along
the drift from Renaissance to Reformation, from Italy to Ger-

many, stride two gigantic protagonists, the rogue and the fool.
In the conflicts of humanistic learning and empirical experience,
the war between theology and science, a literature is evolved
which has the expansiveness of the picaresque and the inclu-
siveness of satire. It is the age of Erasmus, Brandt, Rabelais, and
Cervantes. It is a time to cry "Ducdame" and call all fools into
a circle.'[6]

That circle is the magic circle of comedy, and the fool is the
comic character par excellence. To be foolish is, above all, to be
risible and if, as Aristotle said, laughter is the exclusive property
of man, the fool is the most human of us all. Indeed, that is
precisely what he will claim when he addresses the sixteenth-
century world. His boast is Falstaff's:

The brain of this foolish, compounded clay, man, is not able to invent anything
that tends to laughter more than I invent or is invented on me: I am not only
witty in myself, but the cause that wit is in other men.

[*2 Henry IV*, I ii 8–12]

Witty and *wit*, however, are equivocal terms; they may refer
either to laughter or to wisdom, to the fool or to the wise. The
function of the professional fool, in imitation of the natural fool,
is to create laughter – a role that Falstaff sees himself in when
he calculates how he will be able to 'devise enough matter out
of this Shallow to keep Prince Harry in continual laughter'. The
function of the wise man, on the other hand, is to teach the
truth. Out of the paradoxical concepts of Kempis and Cusanus,
the Renaissance developed the oxymoronic concept of the wise
fool, who embodies these paradoxes and capitalises upon the
equivocation in the word *wit*. He manages, that is, to present
truth by means of comedy, claiming to be wise when he laughs
and to teach us wisdom when he causes laughter in us. The
Renaissance cult of the fool is humanism on a holiday, much as
the medieval *fête des fous* was religion on a holiday; but the
praisers of folly saw that there was in the holiday world as much
truth as there was in the working-day world. James Joyce is said
once to have emended *in vino veritas* to *in risu veritas*, and, though
the fool of the humanists would hate to see anything substituted
for wine, he would agree that laughter is also a source of truth.

The fool laughs because he is human, because he takes a profound delight in life, and because, like one of Meredith's 'very
penetrative, very wicked imps', he can see the folly of the wise.
For a world that was prepared to consider his laughter irrespon-
sible, the fool of the Renaissance reiterated Horace's rhetorical
question: 'ridentem dicere verum quid vetat?' ['Why should
laughter not convey truth?': *Satires*, ı 1 24 –Ed.]

That he teaches by laughing is also significant of his epoch;
for though the didactic potentialities of comedy and laughter,
demonstrated at least as early as Aristophanes, were accepted
by classical antiquity, the Middle Ages seem to have been less
certain of them. At times they did assign a moral or didactic
role to comedy – as, for example, in the dramas of Hrotsvitha
– but comedy does not here so much indicate humor as describe
a genre. There are, of course, certain passages in the plays of
the Abbess of Gandersheim that are intended to provoke laughter, but it is doubtful if she thought such passages taught very
much wisdom. It was her comic plots that were intended to
teach, and her scenes of humor seem closer to what we should
call mere 'comic relief' from the intensity of the moral lesson.
The whole problem of the medieval attitude toward laughter is,
as Curtius has indicated, a vexing one;[7] but in any event it is
certainly not until the paradoxical concept of the wise fool is
developed that we find any striking examples later than classical
literature of comic laughter teaching. As wisdom and folly
confront each other in the same person, sustained irony becomes
possible for the first time since the classical age, and in the
laughter of fools the voice of wisdom is heard.

Source: extract from *Praisers of Folly: Erasmus, Rabelais,
Shakespeare* (Cambridge, Mass., 1963; London, 1964), pp.4–
13.

NOTES

[Revised and renumbered from the original –Ed.]

1. Erasmus, *The Praise of Folly* (*Encomium Moriae* in the original Latin
version, 1509), as translated by Sir Thomas Chaloner (1549); edited by
Clarence H. Miller for the Early English Text Society (Oxford, 1965), p. 68.

2. Robert Burton, *The Anatomy of Melancholy* (1621), part 2, sec. 3, mem. 8; reprinted in 2 vols (London, 1837): II, pp. 84–5.

3. Erwin Panofsky, 'Renaissance and Renaissances', *Kenyon Review*, VI (1944), pp. 201–36; reproduced in *Renaissance and Renaissances in Western Art* (London, 1970), pp. 42–113.

4. Ernst Cassirer, *Individuum und Kosmos in der Philosophie der Renaissance* (Leipzig, 1927), p. 7.

5. *The Fool: His Social and Literary History* (London, 1935), p. 21.

6. Harry Levin (ed.), *Selected Works of Ben Jonson* (New York, 1938), p. 12.

7. Ernst Robert Curtius, *European Literature and the Latin Middle Ages*; translated from the German original by Willard R. Trask (New York, 1953), pp. 417–35.

Mikhail Bakhtin 'Comedy and Carnival Tradition' (1968)

... Carnival festivities and the comic spectacles and ritual connected with them had an important place in the life of medieval man. Besides carnivals proper, with their long and complex pageants and processions, there was the 'feast of fools' (*festa stultorum*) and the 'feast of the ass'; there was a special free 'Easter laughter' (*risus paschalis*), consecrated by tradition. Moreover, nearly every Church feast had its comic folk aspect, which was also traditionally recognised. Such, for instance, were the parish feasts, usually marked by fairs and varied open-air amusements, with the participation of giants, dwarfs, monsters and trained animals. A carnival atmosphere reigned on days when mysteries and *soties* were produced. This atmosphere also pervaded such agricultural feasts as the harvesting of grapes (*vendange*) which was celebrated also in the city. Civil and social ceremonies and rituals took on a comic aspect as clowns and fools, constant participants in these festivals, mimicked serious rituals such as the tribute rendered to the victors at tournaments, the transfer of feudal rights or the initiation of a knight. Minor occasions were also marked by comic protocol, as for instance the election of a king and queen to preside at a banquet 'for laughter's sake' (*roi pour rire*).

All these forms of protocol and ritual based on laughter and consecrated by tradition existed in all the countries of medieval Europe; they were sharply distinct from the serious official, ecclesiastical, feudal and political cult forms and ceremonials. They offered a completely different, non-official, extra-ecclesiastical and extra-political aspect of the world, of man and of human relations; they built a second world and a second life outside officialdom: a world in which all medieval people participated more or less, in which they lived during a given time of the year. If we fail to take into consideration this two-world condition, neither medieval cultural consciousness nor the culture of the Renaissance can be understood. To ignore or to underestimate the laughing people of the Middle Ages also distorts the picture of European culture's historic development.

This double aspect of the world and of human life existed even at the earliest stages of cultural development. In the folklore of primitive peoples, coupled with the cults which were serious in tone and organisation were other, comic cults which laughed and scoffed at the deity ('ritual laughter'); coupled with serious myths were comic and abusive ones; coupled with heroes were their parodies and doublets. These comic rituals and myths have attracted the attention of folklorists.

But at the early stages of pre-class and pre-political social order it seems that the serious and the comic aspects of the world and of the deity were equally sacred, equally 'official'. This similarity was preserved in rituals of a later period of history. For instance, in the early period of the Roman state the ceremonial of the triumphal procession included on almost equal terms the glorifying and the deriding of the victor. The funeral ritual was also composed of lamenting (glorifying) and deriding the deceased. But in the definitely consolidated state and class structure such an equality of the two aspects became impossible. All the comic forms were transferred, some earlier and others later, to a non-official level. There they acquired a new meaning, were deepened and rendered more complex, until they became the expression of folk consciousness, of folk culture. Such were the carnival festivities of the ancient world, especially the Roman Saturnalias, and such were medieval carnivals. They were, of course, far removed from the primitive community's ritual laughter.

What are the peculiar traits of the comic rituals and spectacles of the Middle Ages? Of course, these are not religious rituals like, for instance, the Christian liturgy to which they are linked by distant genetic ties. The basis of laughter which gives form to carnival rituals frees them completely from all religious and ecclesiastic dogmatism, from all mysticism and piety. They are also completely deprived of the character of magic and prayer; they do not command nor do they ask for anything. Even more, certain carnival forms parody the Church's cult. All these forms are systematically placed outside the Church and religiosity. They belong to an entirely different sphere.

Because of their obvious sensuous character and their strong element of play, carnival images closely resemble certain artistic forms, namely the spectacle. In turn, medieval spectacles often tended toward carnival folk culture, the culture of the market-place, and to a certain extent became one of its components. But the basic carnival nucleus of this culture is by no means a purely artistic form nor a spectacle and does not, generally speaking, belong to the sphere of art. It belongs to the borderline between art and life. In reality, it is life itself, but shaped according to a certain pattern of play.

In fact, carnival does not know footlights, in the sense that it does not acknowledge any distinction between actors and spectators. Footlights would destroy a carnival, as the absence of footlights would destroy a theatrical performance. Carnival is not a spectacle seen by the people; they live in it, and everyone participates because its very idea embraces all the people. While carnival lasts, there is no other life outside it. During carnival time life is subject only to its laws, that is, the laws of its own freedom. It has a universal spirit; it is a special condition of the entire world, of the world's revival and renewal, in which all take part. Such is the essence of carnival, vividly felt by all its participants. It was most clearly expressed and experienced in the Roman Saturnalias, perceived as a true and full, though temporary, return of Saturn's golden age upon earth. The tradition of the Saturnalias remained unbroken and alive in the medieval carnival, which expressed this universal renewal and was vividly felt as an escape from the usual official way of life.

Clowns and fools, which often figure in Rabelais's novel, are characteristic of the medieval culture of humor. They were the constant, accredited representatives of the carnival spirit in everyday life out of carnival season. Like Triboulet at the time of Francis I, they were not actors playing their parts on a stage, as did the comic actors of a later period, impersonating Harlequin, Hanswurst, etc., but remained fools and clowns always and wherever they made their appearance. As such they represented a certain form of life, which was real and ideal at the same time. They stood on the borderline between life and art, in a peculiar mid-zone as it were; they were neither eccentrics nor dolts, neither were they comic actors.

Thus carnival is the people's second life, organised on the basis of laughter. It is a festive life. Festivity is a peculiar quality of all comic rituals and spectacles of the Middle Ages.

All these forms of carnival were also linked externally to the feasts of the Church. (One carnival did not coincide with any commemoration of sacred history or of a saint but marked the last days before Lent, and for this reason was called *Mardi gras* or *carême-prenant* in France and *Fastnacht* in Germany.) Even more significant is the genetic link of these carnivals with ancient pagan festivities, agrarian in nature, which included the comic element in their rituals.

The feast (every feast) is an important primary form of human culture. It cannot be explained merely by the practical conditions of the community's work, and it would be even more superficial to attribute it to the physiological demand for periodic rest. The feast had always an essential, meaningful philosophical content. No rest period or breathing spell can be rendered festive per se; something must be added from the spiritual and ideological dimension. They must be sanctioned not by the world of practical conditions but by the highest aims of human existence, that is, by the world of ideals. Without this sanction there can be no festivity.

The feast is always essentially related to time, either to the recurrence of an event in the natural (cosmic) cycle, or to biological or historic timeliness. Moreover, through all the stages of historic development feasts were linked to moments of crisis, of breaking points in the cycle of nature or in the life of society and man. Moments of death and revival, of change and renewal always led to a festive perception of the world. These moments, expressed in concrete form, created the peculiar character of the feasts.

In the framework of class and feudal political structure this specific character could be realised without distortion only in the carnival and in similar market-place festivals. They were the second life of the people, who for a time entered the utopian realm of community, freedom, equality and abundance.

On the other hand, the official feasts of the Middle Ages, whether ecclesiastic, feudal or sponsored by the state, did not lead the people out of the existing world order and created no second life. On the contrary, they sanctioned the existing pattern of things and reinforced it. The link with time became formal; changes and moments of crisis were relegated to the past. Actually, the original feast looked back at the past and used the past to consecrate the present. Unlike the earlier and purer feast, the official feast asserted all that was stable, unchanging, perennial: the existing hierarchy, the existing religious, political and moral values, norms and prohibitions. It was the triumph of a truth already established, the predominant truth that was put forward as eternal and indisputable. This is why the tone of the official feast was monolithically serious and why the element of laughter was alien to it. The true nature of human festivity was betrayed and distorted. But this true festive character was indestructible; it had to be tolerated and even legalised outside the official sphere and had to be turned over to the popular sphere of the market-place.

As opposed to the official feast, one might say that carnival celebrated temporary liberation from the prevailing truth and from the established order; it marked the suspension of all hierarchical rank, privileges, norms and prohibitions. Carnival was the true feast of time, the feast of becoming, change and renewal. It was hostile to all that was immortalised and completed.

The suspension of all hierarchical precedence during carnival time was of particular significance. Rank was especially evident during official feasts; everyone was expected to appear in the full regalia of his calling, rank and merits, and to take the place corresponding to his position. It was a consecration of inequality. On the contrary, all were considered equal during carnival. Here, in the town square, a special form of free and familiar contact reigned among people who were usually divided by the barriers of caste, property, profession and age. The hierarchical background and the extreme corporative and caste divisions of the medieval social order were exceptionally strong. Therefore such free, familiar contacts were deeply felt and formed an essential element of the carnival spirit. People were, so to speak, reborn for new, purely human, relations. These truly human relations were not only a fruit of imagination or abstract thought; they were experienced. The utopian ideal and the realistic merged in this carnival experience, unique of its kind.

This temporary suspension, both ideal and real, of hierarchical rank created during carnival time a special type of communication impossible in everyday life. This led to the creation of special forms of market-place speech and gesture, frank and free, permitting no distance between those who came in contact with each other and liberating from norms of etiquette and decency imposed at other times. A special carnivalesque, market-place style of expression was formed which we find abundantly represented in Rabelais's novel.

During the century-long development of the medieval carnival, prepared by thousands of years of ancient comic ritual, including the primitive Saturnalias, a special idiom of forms and symbols was evolved – an extremely rich idiom that expressed the unique yet complex carnival experience of the people. This experience, opposed to all that was ready-made and completed, to all pretence at immutability, sought a dynamic expression; it demanded ever changing, playful, undefined forms. All the symbols of the carnival idiom are filled with this pathos of change and renewal, with the sense of the gay relativity of prevailing truths and authorities. We find here a characteristic logic, the peculiar logic of the 'inside out' (à l'envers), of the 'turnabout', of a continual shifting from top to bottom, from front to rear, of numerous parodies and travesties, humiliations, profanations, comic crownings and uncrownings. A second life, a second world of folk culture is thus constructed; it is to a certain extent a parody of the extra-carnival life, a 'world inside out'. We must stress, however, that the carnival is far distant from the negative and formal parody of modern times. Folk humor denies, but it revives and renews at the same time. Bare negation is completely alien to folk culture.

Our introduction has merely touched upon the exceptionally rich and original idiom of carnival forms and symbols. The principal aim of the present work is to understand this half-forgotten idiom, in so many ways obscure to us. For it is precisely this idiom which was used by Rabelais, and without it we would fail to understand his system of images. This carnival imagery was also used, although differently and to a different degree, by

Erasmus, Shakespeare, Lope de Vega, Guevara and Quevedo, by the German 'literature of fools' (*Narren-literatur*) and by Hans Sachs, Fischart, Grimmelshausen and others. Without an understanding of it, therefore, a full appreciation of Renaissance and grotesque literature is impossible. Not only belles lettres but the utopias of the Renaissance and its conception of the universe itself were deeply penetrated by the carnival spirit and often adopted its forms and symbols.

Let us say a few initial words about the complex nature of carnival laughter. It is, first of all, a festive laughter. Therefore it is not an individual reaction to some isolated 'comic' event. Carnival laughter is the laughter of all the people. Second, it is universal in scope: it is directed at all and everyone, including the carnival's participants. The entire world is seen in its droll aspect, in its gay relativity. Third, this laughter is ambivalent: it is gay, triumphant, and at the same time mocking, deriding. It asserts and denies, it buries and revives. Such is the laughter of carnival.

Let us enlarge upon the second important trait of the people's festive laughter: that it is also directed at those who laugh. The people do not exclude themselves from the wholeness of the world. They, too, are incomplete, they also die and are revived and renewed. This is one of the essential differences of the people's festive laughter from the pure satire of modern times. The satirist whose laughter is negative places himself above the object of his mockery, he is opposed to it. The wholeness of the world's comic aspect is destroyed, and that which appears comic becomes a private reaction. The people's ambivalent laughter, on the other hand, expresses the point of view of the whole world; he who is laughing also belongs to it.

Let us here stress the special philosophical and utopian character of festive laughter and its orientation toward the highest spheres. The most ancient rituals of mocking at the deity have here survived, acquiring a new essential meaning. All that was purely cultic and limited has faded away, but the all-human, universal and utopian element has been retained.

The greatest writer to complete the cycle of the people's carnival laughter and bring it into world literature was Rabelais. His work will permit us to enter into the complex and deep nature of this phenomenon.

The problem of folk humor must be correctly posed. Current literature concerning this subject presents merely gross modernisations. The present-day analysis of laughter explains it either as purely negative satire (and Rabelais is described as a pure satirist), or else as gay, fanciful, recreational drollery deprived of philosophic content. The important point made previously, that folk humor is ambivalent, is usually ignored. ...

SOURCE: extract from the Introduction to *Rabelais and His World* (Russian original, written 1940, published in 1965); English version, translated by Helene Iswolsky (Cambridge, Mass., and London, 1968; paperback edn, 1971), pp. 5–12.

Ian Donaldson   Justice in the Stocks
(1970)

> ... Liberty plucks Justice by the nose,
> The baby bears the nurse, and quite athwart
> Goes all decorum.
>   *Measure for Measure* [I iii 29-31]

'Definitions are hazardous', said Dr Johnson with a wise caution, writing on the subject of comedy in his one hundred and twenty-fifth *Rambler*. Comedy is a living and evolving form, always changing a shade faster than the definitions which pursue it; the wish to circumscribe comedy with a system of theoretical ideas is in itself a somewhat comic ambition, like Walter Shandy's wish to write a *Tristrapaedia* which would prepare his son for every conceivable event that might overtake him during his early life. Yet to recognise the hazards is not necessarily to fall in with the old-fashioned and somewhat magical view that comedy cannot profitably be talked about, that it exists only to be seen and to be laughed at. Like every other form of literature, comedy arouses not only an immediate pleasure but also a legitimate curiosity about the possible sources and organising principles of that pleasure. And to explore, in particular, the comedy of an age other than our own is often to be moved not so much to spontaneous laughter as to questions about laughter. Why, we may wonder, should certain kinds of comedy ever have been thought funny in the first place; why should certain comic scenes (like certain comic stories) recur with such persistence over the years; what, if anything, do such comedies tell us about the society which first enjoyed them; what, if anything, do they tell us about the function of comedy in general?

Here, for example, is one comic situation which reappears in English stage comedy so doggedly and over such a period of time that it is likely to drive us to some speculation. It might be called the discomfiture of the judge. A scene from the fourth act of Vanbrugh's *The Provok'd Wife* will serve to show the basic pattern of joke. The scene has some interest in that it underwent rewriting some time between 1697 and 1725, probably as a result of Jeremy Collier's attack upon Vanbrugh in his *Short View of the Immorality and Profaneness of the English Stage* in 1698. Sir John Brute and his friends, at an advanced stage of a night's toping, are out walking the streets when they meet with a tailor. The tailor is carrying a bundle; in the first version of the play the bundle contains the gown of the local minister of religion; in the revised version – 'to suit the delicacy of the age', as Hazlitt dryly put it – it contains the gown of Lady Brute herself. Sir John promptly put it on; he runs into the watch; fights with them, and is overcome; and is finally led before an amazed Justice of the Peace. For some minutes the supposed Lady Brute allows the Justice's inquisition to proceed, until the questions turn to the behaviour of Sir John himself 'in the grand matrimonial point'. 'Oons!' says Sir John, 'This fellow asks so many impertinent questions! I'gad, *I believe it is the Justice's wife in the Justice's clothes.*' The line was there in the original version, but without the situational relevance to give it full comic force; with the simplest of touches Vanbrugh has now shaped the scene to a classic comic pattern, in which the dignity and inviolability of the law is suddenly subverted by a preposterous hint – its truth or falsehood hardly matters – that beneath the judge's robes is a human being as devious and as fallible as the prisoner in his custody. 'Hark, in thine ear: change places, and, handy-dandy, which is the justice, which is the thief?'

Seventeenth-century rhetoricians had a name for such a moment as this when it occurred in formal debate, a speaker's own accusation (or suspicion) being suddenly turned back against himself by his opponent: this was known as an inversion. But comic inversion may involve more than a mere verbal stroke. Consider some more discomfited judges. Ben Jonson's Justice Overdo dresses as a fool in order to spy out the enormities of Smithfield Fair, but finds himself denounced by his own wife as one of the greatest of the fair's enormities ('Mine own words turned upon me like swords'), beaten, and placed in the stocks (*Bartholomew Fair*, 1614). Richard Brome's Justice Cockbrain, out to do for Covent Garden what 'my Reverent Ancestor *Justice Adam Overdo*' did for Smithfield, follows his suspects into an inn only to be humiliated and clubbed (*Covent Garden Weeded*,

1632). Thomas Shadwell's Sir Humphrey Maggot, Alderman and Justice of the Peace, is carried off by his nephew's crew of roaring boys to an inn, and is finally thrown out again, drunk; when the crew is brought before him for sentence next morning, they remind him of the treasons he uttered in his cups the night before: 'I shall be hang'd', he exclaims, and quickly dismisses the charge (*The Scowrers*, 1690). Henry Fielding's Mr Justice Squeezum, having had two men imprisoned for rapes they did not commit, is himself surprised in a tavern attempting to seduce the principal female witness, and must endure the rebukes of a drunkard named Sotmore: 'Fie upon you, Mr Squeezum! you who are a magistrate, you who are the preserver and executor of our laws, thus to be the breaker of them!' (*Rape Upon Rape; or, the Justice Caught in his own Trap*, 1730). Arthur Wing Pinero's Mr Posket, after a night of escapades, perilous falls, and long-distance running, returns in a dishevelled state to his Magistrate's Court next morning to discover that he must try his companions of the previous night – including his own wife (*The Magistrate*, 1885).

Why do we find this comic pattern so often repeated? One answer might be that such scenes, at their most farcical and primitive level, effect for us a satisfying act of comic revenge against those whose authority we habitually respect and fear; a form of comic play-acting is allowed temporarily to overthrow another form of highly serious play-acting (the administration of justice) on which the stability of society depends. Thus the police, too, become popular objects of comic retribution. Mr Punch, in what is perhaps the most fundamental piece of comedy our society still regularly enjoys, gives thump after thump to constable after constable, and finally hangs the hangman (though originally, we are told, the hangman seems to have had the last word on this matter). John Gay's short play *The Mohocks* (1712) sketches the pattern of comic revenge equally clearly: a gang of street terrorists force the constable and watch to exchange garments with them, and then march these disguised officers of the law off for trial before the unsuspecting Justices of the Peace. Such farcically incompetent officers are the forerunners of the Keystone Cops.

Yet a scene of this kind may also suddenly modulate from

farce into an altogether more complex comic mode which is at
once more compassionate and more moral. In the fifth act of
Bartholomew Fair Jonson leads us brilliantly from the farcical
encounter of priest and puppet to the humanity of the play's
conclusion: '... remember you are but *Adam*, Flesh and blood!
You haue your frailty, forget your other name of *Ouerdoo*, and
inuite vs all to supper.' And in *The Magistrate* Mr Posket makes
the same anguished discovery, that beneath the robes is flesh
and blood: 'I am a man as well as a magistrate.' *Judge not, that
ye be not judged*: such moments as these derive their particular
poignancy from the wit and compassion with which they seem
to recall the gospel sentences on the absurdity of fallible man's
attempting to pass judgement upon his fellows. A further modulation, and we move out of the world of comedy and into that
of tragicomedy, from *Bartholomew Fair* to *Measure for Measure*,
where another righteous judge discovers, to his own perturba-
tion, the man beneath the robes: 'Blood, thou art blood.' Another modulation still, and we are in Lear's world, where
Christ's words (this time on the woman taken in adultery, John
8:7) are driven to a fierce, anarchical conclusion:

> Thou rascal beadle, hold thy bloody hand!
> Why dost thou lash that whore? Strip thine own back;
> Thou hotly lusts to use her in that kind
> For which thou whipp'st her. ...
>
> [IV vi 162–5]

No man is fit to judge another, or to rule another: Lear's vision
is of a tragic stalemate, with beadle and whore, justice and thief,
father and daughters, husband and wife, servant and master,
king and clown standing on a common level, each as good and
as wicked as his fellow, each without virtue enough to command
or humility enough to be subordinate. The sense of levelling
and of deadlock is, for all the obvious, large differences, curi-
ously close to that which is sometimes arrived at by comedy; we
do well to remember how powerfully the two apparently quite
contradictory modes of tragedy and comedy may sometimes
enrich each other by reason of their mutual proximity.

Two very closely related comic principles might be said to be
at work in the scenes we have just looked at. The first, more

broadly farcical element arises largely out of a comic principle which Henri Bergson described as *inversion*, a term which significantly coincides with the old rhetorical term we have already met.[1] Inversion involves a sudden, comic switching of expected roles: prisoner reprimands judge, child rebukes parent, wife rules husband, pupil instructs teacher, master obeys servant. The conventions of Roman New Comedy, with its clever children, wives and servants pitted against dim-witted fathers, pedants, husbands and masters provided generously for comedy of this kind; and the conventions are still strong in Elizabethan comedy. Lyly's comedies, for instance, make constant use of this comic device; in *Mother Bombie* one aged father confesses to another: '... wee are both well serued: the sonnes must bee masters, the fathers gaffers; what wee get together with a rake, they cast abroade with a forke; and wee must wearie our legges to purchase our children armes' [I iii 185-8]. The neat dance of the phrases creates a sense of order and playfulness which contrasts nicely with the weariness and disorder actually being described; Lyly's style continually reassures us that we are to remain within the safe world of comedy. With a similar nimbleness the two servants congratulate each other on their skill in bringing about these reversals:

DROMIO. His knauerie and my wit, should make our masters that are wise, fooles; their children that are fooles, beggars; and vs two that are bond, free.

RISCIO. He to cosin, & I to coniure, would make such alterations, that our masters should serue themselues; the ideots, their children, serue vs; and we to wake our wits betweene them all.   [II i 5-10]

The fathers serve the children, the children serve the bond-servants, the bond-servants alone are free, lords for the day; the entire social pyramid is inverted.

The second and more complex comic principle might be described as *levelling*. Here the emphasis is not so much upon reversal of roles or the triumph of a natural underdog as upon the artificiality of all social distinctions in the face of human passion and incompetence. Fielding is one of the masters of this kind of comedy. In the great social masquerade, he writes in his *Essay on the Knowledge of the Characters of Men*, 'Nature is ever endeavouring to peep forth and show herself; nor can the cardinal, the friar, or the judge, long conceal the sot, the gamester,

or the rake.'[2] Levelling comedy is comedy of unmasking, comedy which reveals unexpected and embarrassing brotherhood
in error, comedy which (temporarily at least) stuns, disables
and humbles its protagonists; comedy which eyes ironically the
proposition that our social superiors are also our moral superiors. Fielding's chambermaid Betty, found by Mrs Tow-wouse
in a compromising position with Mr Tow-wouse, valiantly protests that *her betters are worse than she*: such subversive sentiments
lie at the heart of comedy of this kind. *Our Betters* is the ironical
title of Somerset Maugham's comedy of upper-class life. Yet it
is characteristic of levelling comedy that it explodes in two
directions at once. 'Zbud, I think you men of quality will grow
as unreasonable as the women', protests the shoemaker to the
aristocratic rake, Dorimant, in the first act of Etherege's *The
Man of Mode*; 'You would engross the sins o' the nation; poor
folks can no sooner be wicked, but they're railed at by their
betters.' 'Had the Play remain'd, as I at first intended', says
Gay's beggar ruefully at the end of *The Beggar's Opera*, 'it would
have carried a most excellent moral. 'Twould have shown that
the lower sort of people have their vices in a degree as well as
the rich: And that they are punish'd for them.' And the demure
Mrs Slipslop, sympathetically assuring Lady Booby of the like-
lihood of Joseph Andrews's fondness for her, reminds her that
'Servants have flesh and blood as well as quality'. Levelling
comedy begins with a series of apparent contrasts; between the
morality of high life ('Our Betters') and that of low life; between
the corruption of the city and the pastoral innocence of the
country; between the honesty of plain-dealing and the hypocrisy
of manners; between the strength of the man in office and the
powerlessness of the man out of office; and then quickly proceeds
to demolish the entire artificial structure of contrasts: each man
is as good and as bad, as powerful and as impotent as his fellow,
no place and no style of life will assure us of strength or of virtue,
we are all of us no worse and no better than Our Betters; 'flesh
and blood', we all stand on a common level.

It is not surprising, then, that the comic dramatist should so
often find himself accused of being a social saboteur; for such
comedy characteristically represents society collapsing under
the strain of scandalous and widespread folly and ineptitude,

centred in particular in those traditionally thought to be
society's very pillars. 'If these gentlemen had fairly represented
the average ability of the Justices of the time', remarks Miss
C.V. Wedgwood pertinently of the figure of the JP as represented in Caroline drama, 'it would be hard to understand how
the administration functioned.'³ While in real life we have many
judges who are wise and blameless, in comedy all judges are
scatter-brained and culpable; it was just this *kind* of distortion
which so distressed Jeremy Collier in 1698. Restoration comedy,
Collier argued, is disrespectful to Our Betters. What right, he
asked, has the comic dramatist to treat the clergy and the
aristocracy as though they were the same as everyone else? 'And
has our *Stage* a particular Privilege? Is their *Charter* inlarg'd, and
are they on the same Foot of Freedom with the *Slaves* in the
Saturnalia? Must all Men be handled alike? ... I hope the *Poets*
don't intend to revive the old Project of Levelling, and *Vote*
down the House of *Peers*.'⁴ Such comedy, for Collier, had political implications; he lined the dramatists up with the old political party of the Levellers. Over forty years later, Colley Cibber
was to accuse Fielding of just the same indiscriminate disrespect
to authority in his political burlesque plays. Fielding's plays,
wrote Cibber, 'seem'd to knock all Distinctions of Mankind on
the Head: Religion, Laws, Government, Priests, Judges, and
Ministers, were all laid flat, at the feet of this *Herculean* Satyr-
ists!'⁵ And the long and curious debate about the dangerous
effects of *The Beggar's Opera*, which stretched right through the
eighteenth century, frequently laid the same charge against
John Gay. Thus a writer in *The Gentleman's Magazine* for 15
September 1773 argued that, despite the wit of *The Beggar's
Opera*, the play

is notwithstanding very ill calculated to mend the morals of the common
people, who are pleased to find all ranks and degrees, the highest and most
respectable characters, brought down to a level with themselves. The Beggar's
Opera is, in truth, the Thief's Creed and Common Prayer book, in which he
fortifies himself in the most atrocious Wickedness, from the impunity and
triumph of his great exemplar, Mackheath; and comforts himself, that, notwithstanding he may be hanged for his robbery, he is no worse than his betters.

In private life, the comic dramatist is unlikely to be either an
anarchist or a leveller; Fielding (to take an obvious instance)

happened to be a magistrate himself in his later life, and was a man of generally conservative social beliefs. Yet for all their naïvety, the criticisms just quoted do manage to highlight a major technical problem which faced such a dramatist: namely, how to hint that, behind the cheerfully anarchical society which his comedy depicted, lay a colder, more upright, actual social world to whose forms, hierarchies, law and order he personally gave assent; how to lead the comedy back from a world of cakes and ale to a world in which stewards must play their part; how to banish Falstaff and accept the Lord Chief Justice.

The dramatic formula of the judge-brought-to-justice has survived steadily into modern times: Shaw uses it in *Captain Brassbound's Conversion*, so does Stephen Spender (for tragic purposes) in *Trial of a Judge*, so too does John Mortimer in his play *The Judge*. Our next comic situation has not done so well; and it seems worth asking why. This is the comic triumph of wife over husband. The scene in Jonson's *Epicoene* in which Mrs Otter assaults her husband might be taken as a savage but concise example of this situation; a situation which is given more spacious expression in countless seventeenth-century comedies of shrews and cuckolds, of scolding and horning. However cold such comedies may leave us today, their very frequency in the earlier drama suggests their one-time power to touch their audience's nerve-centre. Shrew comedy, obviously enough, thrives in a society which has fairly formalised ideas about the relative rights, dignities and duties pertaining to the roles of husband and wife. *Epicoene* as a whole, for instance, depends for its full effect upon the premiss that a good wife should be seen and not heard. King James was no doubt expressing a commonplace of the age when he declared 'that silence was an incomparable virtue in a woman',[6] and Volpone had good authority for his fruitless rebuke to Lady Would-be, 'that your highest female grace is silence'.[7] Jonson depends upon this received belief in order to establish the full monstrosity of Lady Haughty and her troop, just as elsewhere in the play he depends upon our agreeing that the use of contraceptives is an unnatural practice. So secure can Jonson be in his knowledge of the way in which his audience is likely to react to his talkative women, that he can afford to give some play to the other side of the question, lending the boisterous Mistress Epicoene some unexpectedly reasonable protestations that women should not be treated as though they were less than human: 'Why, did you thinke you had married a statue? or a motion onely? one of the *French* puppets, with the eyes turn'd with a wire?' Jonson himself noted elsewhere that speech is 'the only benefit man hath to expresse his excellencie of mind over other creatures',[8] and this comedy does not simply add strength to a common belief that women ought to be silent, but at points surprisingly sabotages that belief, generating a feeling of paradox, and allowing us to see the monstrosity not only of a shrew but also of the kind of wife demanded by Morose, a speechless one. Yet it is a paradox which does not finally destroy the premiss on which the play rests, that wives really ought to stay quietly in their places. It was for Ibsen's Nora to demolish that premiss, rejecting the idea of the doll-wife, and startling her husband with the simple words, 'You and I have much to say to each other'. Shrew comedy has never been quite the same since. In 1893 Shaw made a clever but unsuccessful attempt to catch the genre on the rebound. The apparent premiss of *The Philanderer* is the newly received Ibsen view, that it is only reasonable that women enjoy the same rights and freedoms as men: the comedy's first target is the meek and submissive womanly woman. Shaw then springs his characteristic counter-attack, parading the New Woman in her full absurdity, and forcing his audience back to an old-fashioned, pre-Ibsen view of things which they had just prided themselves on rejecting; the nonchalant, cigarette-smoking ladies of the Ibsen Club are the Lady Haughties of their day. The paradox which Jonson's comedy lightly touches is that, after all, wives might indeed be treated with a little more sense of equality; Shaw's paradox is that they might well be treated with a little less. Shaw's paradox, unlike Jonson's, has – for all its cleverness – an air of uncertainty about it, which may reflect not only the uncertainty of Shaw's audiences as to the proper role of women, but also, perhaps, the uncertainty of Shaw himself.

Meredith, we may remember, considered that comedy flourished only in societies which permitted equal dealings between the sexes, where men and women stood upon a common level.[9]

Whether the society which enjoyed *The Way of the World* (a comedy which Meredith gave to clinch this proposition) did in fact encourage a feeling of equality between the sexes seems open to question: one might have supposed that one of the implications of that play was that unless women take exceedingly elaborate precautions they may be reduced to a position of servile dependency upon their husbands. The particular pleasure of the more successful seventeenth-century sex-comedy often seems to arise in fact from a feeling of daring abnormality about the behaviour of the plain-dealing and gaily triumphant heroines, who enjoy an exceptional and often temporary liberty of speech (granted them, sometimes, by reason of their male disguise, as in *As You Like It*), rather than one which is naturally accorded them by their society. Although Rosalind may teasingly instruct Orlando in the conduct of a lover and of a husband, we know that she must soon revert to the meeker role of wife; Celia's agonies continually alert us to the nature of Rosalind's boldness: 'You have simply misused our sex in your love-prate.' Comedy arising out of a society which has more relaxed and egalitarian views about the way in which courtships may be conducted, and about the various rights and duties and proprieties pertaining to the roles of husband and wife, is likely to lose this particular kind of excitement, and sex-comedy is likely to find rather different forms.

The same may be true of other kinds of comedy as well. If the joke about the worsted judge is still current while the jokes about shrews and cuckolds seem faded and at times distasteful, then the reason may lie partly in the relative formality in which certain roles are regarded. Judicial procedures are still conducted with a high degree of dignity, ceremony and formality; the power of a judge is still real, and is still widely regarded with a certain fear; jokes about judges, fictions imagining the destruction of that dignity, ceremony and formality, are, consequently, particularly satisfying. Since the passing of the Married Women's Property Act, the relaxation of the divorce laws, and the gradual arrival of new assumptions about the ways in which wives (and, indeed, husbands) may behave if they wish, comedies about hen-pecked husbands and triumphant wives can look somewhat uninteresting. We write comedies about Our Betters when Our Betters have real power. If such comedies depict an inversion or levelling of the social ranks, this need not mean (as Meredith supposed) that a society is in fact egalitarian, nor (as Collier supposed) that its comic dramatists are intent on undermining the accepted principles of that society. It is possible to be confused by too literal an understanding of the traditional Ciceronian notion that comedy holds a mirror to the age, as Vanbrugh and John Dennis each pointed out independently, and with varying degrees of success, in their replies to the attacks that had been made upon *The Relapse* and *The Man of Mode*.[10] 'The business of Comedy', wrote Vanbrugh, 'is to shew people what they shou'd do, by representing them upon the Stage, doing what they shou'd not. . . .' This is hardly convincing either as a defence of *The Relapse* or as universal truth about comedy; yet it is a useful partial truth, for comedy does often deal in opposites, presenting, so to speak, the anti-types as well as the types of its society. The lunatic governor (such as the one who appears at the end of Chapman's *The Widow's Tears*), the incompetent judge, the mock doctor, the equivocating priest, the hen-pecked husband: such are the familiar and recurrent figures in the comedy of a society which gives a general assent to the necessity of entrusting power to its governors, judges, doctors, priests and husbands. . . .

SOURCE: extract from *The World Upside-Down* (Oxford, 1970), pp. 1–14.

NOTES

[Revised and reorganised from the original – Ed.]

1. Henri Bergson, 'Laughter' (French original, 1899), trans. version in Wylie Sypher (ed.), *Comedy* (New York, 1956), pp. 121–3.

2. Henry Fielding, 'An Essay on the Knowledge of the Characters of Men'; reproduced in W. E. Henley (ed.), *The Complete Works of Henry Fielding*, 16 vols (London, 1903); *Miscellaneous Writings*, I, p. 283.

3. C. V. Wedgwood, 'Social Comedy in the Reign of Charles I', in *Truth and Opinion: Historical Essays* (London and New York, 1960), pp. 194–5.

4. Jeremy Collier, *A Short View of the Immorality and Profaneness of the English Stage* (London, 1698), pp. 175–6.

5. Colley Cibber, *An Apology for the Life of Mr Colley Cibber* (1740); edited by Robert W. Lowe (London, 1889, I, p. 287.

6. *King James His Apophthegms* (1643), p. 12.

7. Ben Jonson, *Volpone*, II iv 76–8.

8. Idem, *Timber; or, Discoveries Made upon Men and Matter* (published 1640), 2031–2; in C.H. Herford and P. and E. Simpson, *Works*, II vols (Oxford, 1925–52), VIII, p. 625.

9. George Meredith, 'An Essay on Comedy . . .' (1877, 1897); reproduced in Sypher (ed.), op. cit. [See extracts in Part Two, above.] Meredith's views were interestingly anticipated by James Beattie, 'Essay on Laughter and Ludicrous Composition' (1764), reproduced in his *Essays* (Edinburgh, 1776), pp. 319–486.

10. Sir John Vanbrugh, 'A Short Vindication of the Relapse and the Provok'd Wife from Immorality and Profaneness' (1698); reproduced in Bonamy Dobrée (ed.), *Complete Works of Sir John Vanbrugh*, 4 vols (London, 1927–28), I, p. 206. John Dennis, 'A Defence of Sir Fopling Flutter' (1722), in E.N. Hooker (ed.), *Critical Works of John Dennis*, 2 vols (Baltimore, Md., 1939–43), II, p. 245.

2. CONCEPTIONS OF COMIC FORM

R. S. Crane 'The Attenuation of Fear, Pity and Indignation in the Plot of *Tom Jones*' (1952)

... In [formulating a] principle for any plot, we must consider three things: (1) the general estimate we are induced to form, by signs in the work, of the moral character and deserts of the hero, as a result of which we tend, more or less ardently, to wish for him either good or bad fortune in the end; (2) the judgements we are led similarly to make about the nature of the events that actually befall the hero or seem likely to befall him, as having either painful or pleasurable consequences for him, and this in greater or less degree and permanently or temporarily; and (3) the opinions we are made to entertain concerning the degree and kind of his responsibility for what happens to him, as being either little or great, and, if the latter, the result either of his acting in full knowledge of what he is doing or of some mistake. The form of a given plot is a function of the particular correlation among these three variables which the completed work is calculated to establish, consistently and progressively, in our minds; and in these terms we may say that the plot of *Tom Jones* has a pervasively comic form. The precise sense, however, in which the form is comic is a rather special one, which needs to be carefully defined.

To begin with, it is obviously a plot in which the complication generates much pain and inner suffering for the hero, as a result of misfortunes which would seem genuinely serious to any good person. He is schemed against by a villain who will not stop even at judicial murder to secure his ends, and, what is worse in his eyes, he loses the good will of the two people whom he most

loves, and loses it as a consequence not simply of the machina-
tions of his enemies but of his own mistaken acts. From near the
beginning until close to the end, moreover, he is made to un-
dergo an almost continuous series of distressing indignities: to
be insulted on the score of his birth, to be forbidden the sight of
Sophia, to see her being pushed into a hated marriage with Blifil
and persecuted when she refuses, to be banished abruptly from
home, to be reduced to poverty and forced to take money from
Lady Bellaston, to be laid in wait for by a press gang, to be
compelled to run a man through in self-defense and finally, in
prison, to be faced with the prospect of a disgraceful death.

The hero, furthermore, to whom all this happens is a naturally good man – not notably virtuous, but, for all his faults, at
least the equal of ourselves and of any other character in the
novel in disinterestedness, generosity and tender benevolent
feeling. These traits are impressed upon us in the third book and
are never obscured even in the worst of Tom's troubles in
London; they are, in fact, revivified for us, just at the point
when we might be most tempted to forget them, by the episodes
of Anderson and of Mrs Miller's daughter. We favor Tom,
therefore, even if we do not admire him, and we wish for him
the good fortune with Allworthy and Sophia which he properly
wishes for himself and which, in terms of his basic moral character, he deserves to get. We follow him through his troubles and
distresses, consequently, with a desire that he will eventually be
delivered from them and reunited to his friend and mistress,
and this all the more when, at the climax of his difficulties, we
see him acting, for the first time, in a way we can entirely
approve; in the end, when our wishes for him are unexpectedly
realised, and to a fuller degree than we had anticipated, we feel
some of the satisfaction which Fielding says [xviii, xiii] was then
felt by the principal characters themselves. 'All were happy, but
those the most who had been most unhappy before. Their
former sufferings and fears gave such a relish to their felicity as
even love and fortune, in their fullest flow, could not have given
without the advantage of such a comparison.'

Having conceived a plot in which so sympathetic a character
is subjected in the complication to experiences so painful, it
would have been relatively easy for Fielding to write a novel

similar in form to his *Amelia*, that is to say, a tragi-comedy of common life designed to arouse and then to dissipate, by a sudden happy resolution, emotions of fear and pity for his hero and of indignation toward his enemies. There is, indeed, an even greater material basis for such an effect in *Tom Jones* than in the later novel: the evils that threaten Tom and the indignities he undergoes are, in the abstract, more serious than anything Booth has to fear, and the same thing is true of the persecutions endured by Sophia as compared with those which Amelia is made to suffer. And yet nothing is more evident than that, whereas the emotions awakened in us by the distresses of Booth and Amelia are the graver emotions of anxiety and compassion that yield what Fielding calls 'the pleasure of tenderness', our feelings for Tom and Sophia, as we anticipate or view in actuality the greater evils that befall them prior to the final discovery, partake only in the mildest degree of this painful quality. We do not actively fear for or pity either of them, and our indignation at the actions of their enemies – even the actions of Blifil – never develops into a sustained punitive response.

Nor is the reason for this hard to find. It is generally the case that whatever tends to minimise our fear in a plot that involves threats of undeserved misfortune for the sympathetic characters tends also to minimise our pity when the misfortune occurs and likewise our indignation against the doers of the evil; and fear for Tom and Sophia as they move toward the successive climaxes of their troubles is prevented from becoming a predominant emotion in the complication of *Tom Jones* chiefly by two things.

The first is our perception, which in each case grows stronger as the novel proceeds, that the persons whose actions threaten serious consequences for the hero and heroine are all persons for whom, though in varying degrees, we are bound to feel a certain contempt. The most formidable of them all is, of course, Blifil. As a villain, however, he is no Iago but merely a clever opportunist who is likely to overreach himself (as the failure of his first schemes shows) and whose power of harm depends entirely on the blindness of Allworthy; he deceives Tom only temporarily and Sophia and Mrs Miller not at all; and after we have seen the display of his personal ineptitude in the proposal scene with

Sophia, we are prepared to wait, without too much active suspense, for his final showing-up. Blifil is too coldly selfish, perhaps, to strike us as positively ridiculous, but in the characters of the other agents of misfortune the comic strain is clear. It is most obvious, needless to say, in Squire Western and his sister: who can really fear that the persecutions directed against the determined and resourceful Sophia by such a blundering pair of tyrants can ever issue in serious harm? For Allworthy, too, in spite of his excellent principles, it is hard for us to maintain entire respect; we should certainly take more seriously his condemnation of Tom in Book VI had we not become accustomed, as a result of earlier incidents in the novel, to smile at a man who could believe in the goodness of the two Blifils and whose pride in his own judgement could make him dispose so precipitously of Jenny and Partridge. There are evident comic traits also in all the persons who cause trouble for Tom and Sophia in the later part of the action: in Dowling, the man always in a hurry; in Lady Bellaston, the great dame who pursues a plebeian with frenzied letters and nocturnal visits to his lodgings; in Lord Fellamar, the half-hearted rake; in Fitzpatrick, the unfaithful but jealous husband who will not believe the evidence of his own eyes. In respect of her relations with Tom, though not otherwise, Sophia, too, must be added to the list, as a virtuous girl with a proper amount of spirit (not to say vanity) whose good resolutions against Tom never survive for long in the presence of her lover. These are all manifestations of the ineffectual or ridiculous in a plot in which the impending events are materially painful; and they contribute, on the principle that we fear less or not at all when the agents of harm to a hero are more or less laughable persons, to induce in us a general feeling of confidence that matters are not really as serious as they appear.

A second ground of security lies in the nature of the probabilities for future action that are made evident progressively as the novel unfolds. From the beginning until the final capitulation of Sophia, the successive incidents constantly bring forth new and unexpected complications, each seemingly fraught with more suffering for Tom than the last; but as we read we instinctively infer from past occurrences to what will probably happen next or in the end; and what steadily cumulates in this way, in spite of the gradual worsening of Tom's situation, is an opinion that, since nothing irreparable has so far happened to him, nothing ever will. In one sense – that which relates to its material events – the action becomes more and more serious as it moves to its climax, in another sense – that which relates to our expectations – less and less serious; and I think that any close reader who keeps in mind the earlier parts of the novel as he attends to the later is inevitably made aware of this, with the result that, though his interest mounts, his fear increasingly declines. We come thus to the first climax in Book VI recalling such things as Jenny's assurance to Allworthy that she will someday make known the whole truth, the sudden reversal of the elder Blifil's sinister plans, the collapse, after initial success, of young Blifil's first scheme against Tom, and Tom's return to favor with Allworthy after the incident of Molly's arrest; and all these memories inevitably operate to check the rise of any long-range apprehensions. And it is the same, too, with the second and apparently much more serious climax at the end of Book XVI, when Tom, dismissed by Sophia, lies in prison awaiting the death of Fitzpatrick, who has been given up by his surgeon: we cannot but remember how, in the affairs of Molly and then of Mrs Waters, Sophia has more than once demonstrated her inability to inflict any great or prolonged punishment on Tom for his sins with other women and how, on the occasion of Allworthy's illness in Book V, the outcome had completely disappointed the gloomy predictions of the doctor.

The attenuation, in these ways, of fear, pity and indignation is a necessary condition of the peculiar comic pleasure which is the form of the plot in *Tom Jones*, but it is only a negative and hence not a sufficient condition. A comic effect of any kind would be impossible if we took Tom's increasingly bad prospects with the same seriousness as he himself takes them; but what in a positive sense makes Fielding's plot comic is the combination of this feeling of security with our perception of the decisive role which Tom's own blunders are made to play, consistently, in the genesis of all the major difficulties into which he is successively brought – always, of course, with the eager assistance of Fortune and of the malice or misunderstanding of others. The importance of this becomes clear when we consider how much trouble he would have spared himself had he not mistaken his seduction by Molly for a seduction of her by him; had he not got drunk when he learned of Allworthy's recovery or fought with Blifil and Thwackum; had he not suggested to Western that he be allowed to plead Blifil's case with Sophia; had he not allowed himself to be seduced by Jenny at Upton; had he not thought that his very love of Sophia, to say nothing of his gallantry, required him 'to keep well' with the lady at the masquerade; and, lastly, had he not accepted so uncritically Nightingale's scheme for compelling her to break off the affair.

The truth is that each successive stage of the plot up to the beginning of the dénouement in Book XVII is precipitated by a fresh act of imprudence or indiscretion on the part of Tom, for which he is sooner or later made to suffer not only in his fortune but his feelings, until in the resolution of each sequence, he discovers that the consequences of his folly are after all not so serious as he has feared. This characteristic pattern emerges, even before the start of the complication proper, in the episode of Tom's relations with Molly and Sophia in Book IV and the first part of Book V; it dominates the prolonged suspense of his relations with Allworthy from the time of the latter's illness to the final discovery; and it determines the course of his troubles with Sophia from Upton to the meeting in London and from the ill-conceived proposal scheme to her sudden surrender at the end.

The comic pleasure all this gives us is certainly not of the same kind as that produced by such classic comic plots as (say) Ben Jonson's *The Silent Woman* or, to take a more extreme instance of the type, his *Volpone*, in which a morally despicable person is made, by reason of his own folly or lapse from cleverness, to suffer a humiliating and, to him, though not to others, painful reversal of fortune. The comedy of Blifil is indeed of this simple punitive kind, but our suspense concerning Blifil is only in a secondary way determinative of the effect of Fielding's novel, and the comedy of Tom and hence of the plot as a whole is of a different sort. It is not simple comedy but mixed, the peculiar power of which depends upon the fact that the mistaken acts of the hero which principally excite our amusement are the acts of a man for whom throughout the plot we entertain sympathetic feelings because of the general goodness of his character: we do not want, therefore, to see him suffer any permanent indignity or humiliation, and we never cease to wish good fortune for him. This favorable attitude, moreover, is not contradicted by anything in the acts themselves from which his trouble springs. We perceive that in successive situations, involving threats to his fortune or peace of mind, he invariably does some imprudent or foolish thing, which cannot fail, the circumstances being what, in our superior knowledge, we see them to be, to result for him in painful embarrassment and regret; but we realise that his blunders arise from no permanent weakness of character but are merely the natural errors of judgement, easily corrigible in the future, of an inexperienced and too impulsively generous and gallant young man. We look forward to the probable consequences of his indiscretions, therefore, with a certain anticipatory reluctance and apprehension – a kind of faint alarm which is the comic analogue of fear; it is some such feeling, I think, that we experience, if only momentarily, when Tom gets drunk and goes into the wood with Molly and when, much later, he sends his proposal letter to Lady Bellaston. We know that trouble, more trouble than the young man either foresees or deserves, is in store for him as a result of what he has done, and since, foolish as he is, we favor him against his enemies, the expectation of his inevitable suffering cannot be purely and simply pleasant.

And yet the expectation is never really painful in any positive degree, and it is kept from becoming so by our counter-expectation, established by the devices I have mentioned, that, however acute may be Tom's consequent sufferings, his mistakes will not issue in any permanent frustration of our wishes for his good. In this security that no genuine harm has been done, we can view his present distresses – as when he anguishes over the wrong he thinks he has done to Molly, or finds Sophia's muff in his bed at Upton, or receives her letter – as the deserved consequences of erroneous actions for which any good man would naturally feel embarrassment or shame. We do not therefore pity him in these moments, for all his self-accusations and cries of despair, but rather laugh at him as a man who has behaved ridiculously or beneath himself and is now being properly punished. And our comic pleasure continues into the subsequent resolving scenes – the discovery of Molly in bed with Square, the meeting with Sophia in London, and the final anti-climax of her agreement to marry him the next morning – when it appears that Tom has after all worried himself overmuch; for we now see that he has been doubly ridiculous, at first in not taking his situation seriously enough and then in taking it more seriously than he should. But Tom is a good man, and we expect him to get better, and so our amused reaction to his sufferings lacks entirely the punitive quality that characterises comedy of the Jonsonian type. If the anticipatory emotion is a mild shudder of apprehension, the climactic emotion – the comic analogue of pity – is a kind of friendly mirth at his expense ('poor Tom', we say to ourselves), which easily modulates, in the happy dénouement, into unsentimental rejoicing at his not entirely deserved good fortune.

This, however, is not quite all; for not only does Tom's final good fortune seem to us at least partly undeserved in terms of his own behavior, but we realise, when we look back from the end upon the long course of the action, that he has, in truth, needed all the luck that has been his. Again and again he has been on the verge of genuinely serious disaster; and, though we expect him to survive and hence do not fear for him in prospect, we perceive, at the resolution of each of his major predicaments, that there has been something of a hair's breadth quality in his escape. The cards have indeed been stacked against him; from the beginning to the ultimate discovery, he has been a young man whose lack of security and imprudence more than offset his natural goodness, living in a world in which the majority of people are ill-natured and selfish, and some of them actively malicious, and in which the few good persons are easily imposed upon by appearances. It is against this background of the potentially serious – more than ever prominent in the London scenes – that the story of Tom's repeated indiscretions is made to unfold, with the result that, though the pleasure remains consistently comic, its quality is never quite that of the merely amiable comedy, based likewise upon the blunders of sympathetic protagonists, of such works as *She Stoops to Conquer* or *The*

Rivals. We are not disposed to feel, when we are done laughing at Tom, that all is right with the world or that we can count on Fortune always intervening, in the same gratifying way, on behalf of the good. . . .

SOURCE: extract from essay, 'The Concept of Plot and the Plot of *Tom Jones*', in R.S. Crane et al. (eds), *Critics and Criticism: Ancient and Modern* (Chicago, 1952; abridged edn, 1957), pp. 78–84.

Susanne Langer   The Comic
Rhythm (1953)

... In comedy the stock figure of the buffoon is an obvious
device for building up the comic rhythm, i.e., the image of
Fortune. But in the development of the art he does not remain
the central figure that he was in the folk theater; the lilt and
balance of life which he introduced, once it has been grasped, is
rendered in more subtle poetic inventions involving plausible
characters, and an *intrigue* (as the French call it) that makes for
a coherent, over-all, dramatic action. Sometimes he remains as
a jester, servant or other subsidiary character whose comments,
silly or witty or shrewd, serve to point the essentially comic
pattern of the action, where the verisimilitude and complexity
of the stage-life threaten to obscure its basic form. Those points
are normally 'laughs'; and that brings us to the aesthetic problem of the joke in comedy.

Because comedy abstracts, and reincarnates for our perception, the motion and rhythm of living, it enhances our vital
feeling, much as the presentation of space in painting enhances
our awareness of visual space. The virtual life on the stage is not
diffuse and only half felt, as actual life usually is: virtual life,
always moving visibly into the future, is intensified, speeded up,
exaggerated; the exhibition of vitality rises to a breaking point,
to mirth and laughter. We laugh in the theater at small incidents
and drolleries which would hardly rate a chuckle off-stage. It is
not for such psychological reasons that we go there to be
amused, nor are we bound by rules of politeness to hide our
hilarity; but these trifles at which we laugh are really funnier
where they occur than they would be elsewhere; they are employed
in the play, not merely brought in casually. They occur where
the tension of dialogue or other action reaches a high point. As
thought breaks into speech – as the wave breaks into foam –
vitality breaks into humor.

Humor is the brilliance of drama, a sudden heightening of
the vital rhythm. A good comedy, therefore, builds up to every

laugh; a performance that has been filled up with jokes at the indiscretion of the comedian or of his writer may draw a long series of laughs, yet leave the spectator without any clear impression of a very funny play. The laughs, moreover, are likely to be of a peculiar sameness, almost perfunctory: the formal recognition of a timely 'gag'.

The amoral character of the comic protagonist goes through the whole range of what may be called the comedy of laughter. Even the most civilised products of this art – plays that George Meredith would honor with the name of 'comedy' because they provoke 'thoughtful laughter' [see Meredith excerpt in Part Two, above – Ed.] – do not present moral distinctions and issues, but only the ways of wisdom and folly. Aristophanes, Menander, Molière – practically the only authors this most exacting of critics admitted as truly comic poets – are not moralists, yet they do not flaunt or deprecate morality; they have, literally, 'no use' for moral principles – that is, they do not use them. Meredith, like practically all his contemporaries, labored under the belief that poetry must teach society lessons, and that comedy was valuable for what it revealed concerning the social order. He tried hard to hold its exposé of foibles and vindication of common sense to an ethical standard; yet in his very efforts to justify its amoral personages he only admitted their amoral nature and their simple relish for life, as when he said: 'The heroines of comedy are like women of the world, not necessarily heartless from being clear-sighted. . . . Comedy is an exhibition of their battle with men, and that of men with them . . . .'

There it is, in a nutshell: the contest of men and women – the most universal contest; humanised, in fact civilised, yet still the primitive joyful challenge, the self-preservation and self-assertion whose progress is the comic rhythm.

This rhythm is capable of the most diverse presentations. That is why the art of comedy grows, in every culture, from casual beginnings – miming, clowning, sometimes erotic dancing – to some special and distinctive dramatic art, and sometimes to many forms of it within one culture, yet never seems to repeat its works. It may produce a tradition of dignified drama, springing from solemn ritual, even funereal, its emotional movement too slow to culminate in humor at any point; then other means have to be found to lend it glamor and intensity. The purest heroic comedy is likely to have no humorous passages at all, but to employ the jester only in an ornamental way reminiscent of tragedy, and in fact to use many techniques of tragedy. It may even seem to transcend the amoral comic pattern by presenting virtuous heroes and heroines. But their virtue is a formal affair, a social asset; as Deane remarked of the French classic heroes, they do not submit to ordinary morality: their morality is 'heroism', which is essentially strength, will and endurance in face of the world.[1] Neither have the divinities of oriental drama any 'ordinary morality'; they are perfect in virtue when they slay and when they spare, their goodness is glory, and their will is law. They are Superman, the Hero, and the basic pattern of their conquest over enemies whose only wickedness is resistance, is the amoral life pattern of fencing with the devil – man against death.

Humor, then, is not the essence of comedy, but only one of its most useful and natural elements. It is also its most problematical element, because it elicits from the spectators what appears to be a direct emotional response to persons on the stage, in no wise different from their response to actual people: amusement, laughter.

The phenomenon of laughter in the theater brings into sharp focus the whole question of the distinction between emotion symbolically presented and emotion directly stimulated; it is, indeed, a *pons asinorum* of the theory that this distinction is radical, because it presents us with what is probably the most difficult example. The audience's laugh at a good play is, of course, self-expressive and betokens a 'lift' of vital feeling in each laughing person. Yet it has a different character from laughter in conversation, or in the street when the wind carries off a hat with the 'hair-do' attached, or in the 'laugh house' at an amusement park where the willing victims meet distorting mirrors and things that say 'boo'. All these laughs of daily life are direct responses to separate stimuli; they may be as sporadic as the jokes bandied in a lively company, or may be strung along purposely like the expected and yet unforeseen events in the 'laugh house', yet they remain so many personal encounters that seem funny only if one is in the mood for them. Sometimes we reject witticisms and are bored with tricks and clowning.

It is different in the theater: the play possesses us and breaks our mood. It does not change it, but simply abrogates it. Even if we come in a jovial mood, this does not notably increase our appreciation of humor in the play, for the humor in a good comedy does not strike us directly. What strikes us directly is the dramatic illusion, the stage action as it evolves; and the joke, instead of being as funny as our personal response would make it, seems as funny as its occurrence in the total action makes it. A very mild joke in just the right place might score a big laugh. The action culminates in a witticism, an absurdity, a surprise; the spectators laugh. But after their outburst there is not the letdown that follows an ordinary laugh, because the play moves on without the breathing spell we usually give our own thought and feeling after a joke. The action carries over from one laugh to another, sometimes fairly far spaced; people are laughing *at the play*, not at a string of jokes.

Humor in comedy (as, indeed, in all humorous art) belongs to the work, not to our actual surroundings; and if it is borrowed from the actual world, its appearance in the work is what really makes it funny. Political or topical allusions in a play amuse us because they are *used*, not because they refer to something intrinsically very comical. This device of playing with things from actual life is so sure to bring laughs that the average comic writer and improvising comedian overdo it to the point of artistic ruin; hence the constant flood of 'shows' that have immense popularity but no dramatic core, so they do not outlive the hour of their passing allusions.

Real comedy sets up in the audience a sense of general exhilaration, because it presents the very image of 'livingness' and the perception of it is exciting. Whatever the story may be, it takes the form of a temporary triumph over the surrounding world, complicated, and thus stretched out, by an involved succession of coincidences. This illusion of life, the stage-life, has a rhythm of feeling which is not transmitted to us by separate successive stimulations, but rather by our perception of its entire *Gestalt* – a whole world moving into its own future. The 'livingness' of the human world is abstracted, composed and presented to us; with it the high points of the composition that are illuminated by humor. They belong to the life we see, and our laugh belongs to the theatrical exhilaration, which is universally human and impersonal. It is not what the joke happens to mean to us that measures our laughter, but what the joke does in the play.

For this reason we tend to laugh at things in the theater that we might not find funny in actuality. The technique of comedy often has to clear the way for its humor by forestalling any backsliding into 'the world of anxious interest and selfish solicitude'. It does this by various devices – absurd coincidences, stereotyped expressions of feeling (like the clown's wails of dismay), a quickened pace of action, and other unrealistic effects which serve to emphasise the comic structure. As Professor Fergusson said, 'when we understand a comic convention we see the play with godlike omniscience.... When Scaramouche gets a beating, we do not feel the blows, but the idea of a beating, at that moment, strikes us as funny. If the beating is too realistic, if it breaks the light rhythm of thought, the fun is gone, and the comedy destroyed.'[2]

That 'light rhythm of thought' is the rhythm of life; and the reason it is 'light' is that all creatures love life, and the symbolisation of its impetus and flow makes us really aware of it. The conflict with the world whereby a living being maintains its own complex organic unity is a delightful encounter; the world is as promising and alluring as it is dangerous and opposed. The feeling of comedy is a feeling of heightened vitality, challenged wit and will, engaged in the great game with Chance. The real antagonist is the World. Since the personal antagonist in the play is really that great challenger, he is rarely a complete villain: he is interesting, entertaining, his defeat is a hilarious success but not his destruction. There is no permanent defeat and permanent human triumph except in tragedy; for nature must go on if life goes on, and the world that presents all obstacles also supplies the zest of life. In comedy, therefore, there is a general trivialisation of the human battle. Its dangers are not real disasters, but embarrassment and loss of face. That is why comedy is 'light' compared with tragedy, which exhibits an exactly opposite tendency to general exaggeration of issues and personalities.

The same impulse that drove people, even in prehistoric times, to enact fertility rites and celebrate all phases of their biological existence, sustains their eternal interest in comedy. It is in the nature of comedy to be erotic, risqué and sensuous if not sensual, impious and even wicked. This assures it a spontaneous emotional interest, yet a dangerous one: for it is easy and tempting to command an audience by direct stimulation of feeling and fantasy, not by artistic power. But where the formulation of feeling is really achieved, it probably reflects the whole development of mankind and man's world, for feeling is the intaglio image of reality. The sense of precariousness that is the typical tension of light comedy was undoubtedly developed in the eternal struggle with chance that every farmer knows only too well – with weather, blights, beasts, birds and beetles. The embarrassments, perplexities and mounting panic which characterise that favorite genre, comedy of manners, may still reflect the toils of ritual and taboo that complicated the caveman's existence. Even the element of aggressiveness in comic action serves to develop a fundamental trait of the comic rhythm – the deep cruelty of it, as all life feeds on life. There is no biological truth that feeling does not reflect, and that good comedy, therefore, will not be prone to reveal.

But the fact that the rhythm of comedy is the basic rhythm of life does not mean that biological existence is the 'deeper meaning' of all its themes, and that to understand the play is to interpret all the characters as symbols and the story as a parable, a disguised rite of spring or fertility magic, performed four hundred and fifty times on Broadway. The stock characters are probably symbolic both in origin and in appeal. There are such independently symbolic factors, or residues of them, in all the arts, but their value for art lies in the degree to which their significance can be 'swallowed' by the single symbol, the art work. Not the derivation of personages and situations, but of the rhythm of 'felt life' that the poet puts upon them, seems to me to be of artistic importance: the essential comic feeling, which is the sentient aspect of organic unity, growth and self-preservation.

SOURCE: extract from *Feeling and Form* (New York, 1953; London, 1953), pp. 344–50.

NOTES

[Abbreviated and reorganised from the original –Ed.]

1. C.V. Deane, *Dramatic Theory and the Rhymed Heroic Play* (London, 1931), p. 336.
2. Francis Fergusson, *The Idea of a Theater* (Princeton, N.J., 1949), pp. 178-9.

Friedrich Dürrenmatt 'Comedy and the Modern World' (1958)

... the task of art, in so far as art can have a task at all, and hence also the task of drama today, is to create something concrete, something that has form. This can be accomplished best by comedy. Tragedy, the strictest genre in art, presupposes a formed world. Comedy – in so far as it is not just satire of a particular society as in Molière – supposes an unformed world: a world being made and turned upside down, a world about to fold like ours. Tragedy overcomes distance; it can make myths originating in times immemorial seem like the present to the Athenians. But comedy creates distance; the attempt of the Athenians to gain a foothold in Sicily is translated by comedy into the birds undertaking to create their own empire before which the gods and men will have to capitulate. How comedy works can be seen in the most primitive kind of joke, in the dirty story, which, though it is of very dubious value, I bring up only because it is the best illustration of what I mean by creating distance. The subject of the dirty story is the purely sexual, which, because it is purely sexual, is formless and without objective distance. To give form the purely sexual is transmuted, as I have already mentioned, into the dirty joke. Therefore this type of joke is a kind of original comedy, a transposition of the sexual on to the plain of the comical. In this way it is possible today, in a society dominated by John Doe, to talk in an accepted way about the purely sexual. In the dirty story it becomes clear that the comical exists in forming what is formless, in creating order out of chaos.

The means by which comedy creates distance is the conceit. Tragedy is without conceit. Hence there are few tragedies whose subjects were invented. By this I do not mean to imply that the ancient tragedians lacked inventive ideas of the sort that are written today, but the marvel of their art was that they had no need of these inventions, of conceits. That makes all the difference. Aristophanes, on the other hand, lives by conceits. The stuff of his plays are not myths but inventions, which take place not in the past but the present. They drop into their world like bomb-shells which, by throwing up huge craters of dirt, change the present into the comic and thus scatter the dirt for everyone to see. This, of course, does not mean that drama today can only be comical. Tragedy and comedy are but formal concepts, dramatic attitudes, figments of the aesthetic imagination which can embrace one and the same thing. Only the conditions under which each is created are different, and these conditions have their basis only in small part in art.

Tragedy presupposes guilt, despair, moderation, lucidity, vision, a sense of responsibility. In the Punch-and-Judy show of our century, in this back-sliding of the white race, there are no more guilty and, also, no responsible men. It is always, 'We couldn't help it' and 'We didn't really want that to happen'. And indeed, things happen without anyone in particular being responsible for them. Everything is dragged along and everyone gets caught somewhere in the sweep of events. We are all collectively guilty, collectively bogged down in the sins of our fathers and of our forefathers. We are the offspring of children. That is our misfortune, but not our guilt: guilt can exist only as a personal achievement, as a religious deed. Comedy alone is suitable for us. Our world has led to the grotesque as well as to the atom bomb, and so it is a world like that of Hieronymus Bosch whose apocalyptic paintings are also grotesque. But the grotesque is only a way of expressing in a tangible manner, of making us perceive physically, the paradoxical, the form of the unformed, the face of a world without face; and just as in our thinking today, we seem to be unable to do without the concept of the paradox, so also in art, and in our world which at times seems still to exist only because the atom bomb exists: out of fear of the bomb.

But the tragic is still possible even if pure tragedy is not. We can achieve the tragic out of comedy. We can bring it forth as a frightening moment, as an abyss that opens suddenly; indeed, many of Shakespeare's tragedies are already really comedies out of which the tragic arises.

After all this the conclusion might easily be drawn that comedy is the expression of despair, but this conclusion is not inevitable. To be sure, whoever realises the senselessness, the hopelessness of this world, might well despair, but this despair is not a result of this world. Rather it is an answer given by an individual to this world; another answer would be not to despair, would be an individual's decision to endure this world in which we live like Gulliver among the giants. He also achieves distance, he also steps back a pace or two who takes measure of his opponent, who prepares himself to fight his opponent or to escape him. It is still possible to show man as a courageous being.

In truth this is a principal concern of mine. The blind man, Romulus, Übelohe, Akki, are all men of courage. The lost world-order is restored within them; the universal escapes my grasp. I refuse to find the universal in a doctrine. The universal for me is chaos. The world (hence the stage which represents this world) is for me something monstrous, a riddle of misfortunes which must be accepted but before which one must not capitulate. The world is far bigger than any man, and perforce threatens him constantly. If one could but stand outside the world, it would no longer be threatening. But I have neither the right nor the ability to be an outsider to this world. To find solace in poetry can also be all too cheap; it is more honest to retain one's human point of view. Brecht's thesis, that the world is an accident, which he developed in his *Street Scene* where he shows how this accident happened, may yield – as it in fact did – some magnificent theatre; but he did it by concealing most of the evidence! Brecht's thinking is inexorable, because inexorably there are many things he will not think about.

And lastly it is through the conceit, through comedy, that the anonymous audience becomes possible as an audience, becomes a reality to be counted on, and also one to be taken into account. The conceit easily transforms the crowd of theatre-goers into a mass which can be attacked, deceived, outsmarted into listening to things it would otherwise not so readily listen to. Comedy is a mouse-trap in which the public is easily caught and in which it will get caught over and over again. Tragedy, on the other hand, predicated a true community, a kind of community whose existence in our day is but an embarrassing fiction. Nothing is more ludicrous, for instance, than to sit and watch the mystery plays of the Anthroposophists when one is not a participant.

SOURCE: extract from 'Preface: Problems of the Theatre', in *Four Plays*, *1957–62*, translated by Gerhard Nellhaus (London, 1964), pp. 32–5; the 'Preface' was first published (in this translation) as an essay in *Tulane Drama Review*, III (1958), pp. 3–26.

Eric Bentley 'On the Other Side of Despair' (1964)

1. 'I WAS ONLY JOKING'

When a person vehemently denies something that has not been affirmed, we wonder why he goes to the trouble, and we conclude that expressly what he is denying is true. It is not surprising that this form of no-that-means-yes should turn up frequently on the psychiatric couch where the patient's whole problem lies in his unwillingness to affirm what he knows is so. But in this, as in other respects, the man on the couch is only confronting a possibly acute case of a certainly universal complaint.

Now, instead of using the word no, a patient may burst out laughing. If he should also spell out in words what the laughter has said in grimaces and noise, he would say: 'What you just said is fantastic! You can't be serious! I can't let you find me out like that. Please observe that not only am I nothing daunted; I am daunting you with a laughter which, as you know from your psychological researches, signifies victory and scorn!' Unfortunately, if like most American patients, this patient has done a little psychological reading himself, he knows that strenuous disclaimers are read as confessions of guilt.

Such laughter, far from being confined to clinical situations, is common in all social intercourse. Indeed we have stumbled here upon one of the basic functions of laughter generally, and of all publicly displayed gaiety, frivolity, flippancy, and so on. Even commoner than this 'You can't be serious!' is: 'But I was only joking!' And an interesting variant on this takes place when one's companion refuses to ignore the serious intent and one retorts: 'Can't you take a joke?' conceding the point by an aggrieved and anxious tone.

We have seen that surprisingly blunt aggressions can be undertaken just because of that: 'But it isn't serious' – '*ma non è una cosa seria*', in Pirandello's phrase – which the farce convention carries with it. But then, farce is only serious to the extent that the hostility is felt, and not to the extent of a conviction that the hostility is justified. Comedy brings with it such serious judgements that, but for the disclaimers, a comic play would invite description as a 'powerful indictment' or a 'shocking disclosure'. This is only another way of saying what I have intimated already: that if comedy loses its frivolous tone it becomes non-comic social drama.

Comedy takes over the grave and gay manner of farce. It is the opposing element, the subterranean and eruptive element, that is different. In farce what lies beneath the surface is pure aggression, which gets no moral justification, and asks none. Aggression is common to farce and comedy, but, while in farce it is mere retaliation, in comedy it is might backed by the conviction of right. In comedy, the anger of farce is backed by the conscience.

The ethical difference brings with it quite different emotional colors. Farce offers the one simple pleasure: the pleasure of hitting one's enemy in the jaw without getting hit back. The disapproval expressed in comedy offers a wide range of emotional possibilities, corresponding to the different temperaments that do the disapproving. A man can disapprove almost without disapproving, delicately, saucily, ambiguously, like Congreve; or, like Congreve's contemporary, Jonathan Swift, he can disapprove balefully, searingly, agonisingly.

Many discussions of the comic embrace the Congreves of the art but not the Swifts. Swift, to be sure, was not a playwright, and writers of stage comedy have perhaps nearly always leaned more to Congreve's side than Swift's. Yet this could be because most of them are mediocre. When we take comedy at its admitted greatest – in Machiavelli, or Jonson, or Shakespeare, or Molière – we find the dark undercurrent at its fastest and most powerful. There is no exact terminology to deal with these phenomena, so I will choose the most everyday words and say that what we get ranges between the poles of *bitterness* and *sadness*. Bitterness we know from satire outside the drama, from Juvenal, from Swift. Among the dramatists, Machiavelli and Jonson are bitter. Molière and Shakespeare have bitterness in their repertoire, yet theirs is not predominantly a bitter comedy:

it is sweetly melancholy, and at moments overwhelmingly sad.

Now all mirth ... has bitter as well as sweet springs. It is just that, in farce, the bitterness is never allowed to come flooding to the surface. The water we drink in a farce has, as it were, the merest tinge of bitterness, suggesting that there is more beneath, yes, but not destroying the sweet flavor. The violence of W.C. Fields and Harpo Marx and Charlie Chaplin is there but we are prevented by very clear means from 'taking it seriously' and linking it with the violence of Al Capone or Hitler. Nor in farce can we ever be in the mood to feel sorry for the victims. We are having too good a time doing the victimising. Toward both the attacker and the attacked farce is as unemotional as it is unreflective. Precisely that anti-emotional attitude which Bergson attributes to the comic in general belongs, as I see it, to farce in particular. Farce, not comedy, is 'unfeeling'. Conversely, the bitterness and sadness that so readily come to the surface constitute our first, best evidence that in comedy feeling is not only present but abundant.

Farce affords an escape from living, a release from the pressures of today, a regression to the irresponsibility of childhood. The comic sense, as against the farcical impulse, tries to deal with living, with the pressures of today, with the responsibilities of adulthood. Its (in so many ways) dual character presupposes in the comic artist a dual equipment: on the one hand, a 'lust for life', an 'evolutionary appetite', an eagerness and zest in sheer being, and on the other, a keen and painful awareness of the obstacles in the path, the resistances and recalcitrancies, the trials by fire and water, the dragons, forests and caves that menace us, and the thickets and swamps in which we flounder.

Comedy has this in common with farce: in the end it decides to look the other way. But there is a difference. Comedy has in the meantime looked the right way. Comedy has seen; has taken note; and has not forgotten. Farce all takes place well to this side of despair, brashly, cockily, sophomorically. Comedy takes place on the other side of despair. It is an adult genre. What Joseph Conrad called the shadow-line has been crossed.

In farce we hit back at our oppressor and, in so doing, draw on the primitive, childish sources of pleasure. No pleasure can be purer and more unequivocal than such draughts from the primordial spring. Our experience of comedy, in being more subtle, is also more mixed. To describe and appraise it one perforce uses for purposes of comparison, not farce, but tragedy.

2. 'LET'S NOT GO INTO THAT!'

'Tragedy', said Sir Philip Sidney, 'openeth the greatest wounds and sheweth forth the ulcers that are covered with tissue.' The metaphor conveys the directness of tragedy's relation to pain. Now the plain man's notion that comedy has no such direct relation to pain is correct. The plain man goes wrong only if he assumes that comedy has nothing to do with pain at all.

The further implication of the 'I was only joking!' is: 'Let's not go into that: this is a comedy!' Such an implication may be located in the comic tone as such. Byron is spelling the point out when he says: 'And if I laugh at any mortal thing. 'Tis that I may not weep.' 'Let's not go into that' means: 'That won't bear going into.' Here we have a pessimism that is blacker than tragedy, for tragedy presupposes that everything can be gone into.

Going into everything – plunging into every dark abyss – tragedy brings us to the point of vertigo. Admittedly, comedy does not. The intimation of pain is there, but, in this art, appearances must be maintained, the texture must not lose its lightness. Or not for long.

In great comedy the convention of gaiety is from time to time in danger. Some critics get quite nervous about the fact, and begin to wonder if this is really comedy any more. Mozart's *Così fan tutte*, for instance. That one of the ladies begins to fall in love in earnest and to sing with genuine passion has caused raised eyebrows. Isn't it a violation of comic convention? I would ask, rather: is it not one of the things that lifts *Così fan tutte* above the innumerable works in which convention is not violated? Anyone, after all, can refrain from violating convention.

An example from English drama – a different kind of example – is the Celia scene in *Volpone*. To see Volpone cheating rascals, to see a cheat cheating other cheats, is within the usual bounds of comedy. To see him seducing a truly virtuous wife with the help of her knave of a husband is something else again. Respecters of stability in conventions, moral and aesthetic, may disapprove, but to my mind it is just such touches that make Jonson a great writer of comedy. It is even possible that Jonson himself, priding himself on correctness of theory, would have wilted under 'conventional' criticisms. Jonson's comic genius is by no means contained in his theories. There is tension within the plays between the author's conscious and always highly proper ideas and his deep sense of chaos. Such a tension is far more productive than either the ideas or the sense of chaos alone. Comedy rises through such tensions to grandeur and to greatness.

After Mozart and Ben Jonson, let me cite Molière. He had his own form of 'Let's not go into that.' It is this: 'I'd better end this comedy fast, or it may not remain a comedy'. At the end of *The Would-be Gentleman*, M. Jourdain is no longer merely eccentric or wilful, he is demented. The end of the play spares us the unhappy consequences. The ending of *Tartuffe* is only slightly different. Its foundation is: 'This comedy will have a tragic ending unless the king intervenes at once.' Historical scholars like to remind us what a good monarchist Molière was. But he was an even better dramatist. Happy endings are always ironical (like everything that is happy in comedies), and Molière has made the irony poignant. It is only a step from here to *The Beggar's Opera* where a happy ending is openly mocked. There is a danger to comedy in such open mockery. The sticklers for strict adherence to conventions have this much right on their side: when the convention of comedy is defied beyond a certain point, comedy will give place to something else. I would only add that this is not necessarily a misfortune, and in the next chapter [not excerpted here – Ed.] I shall try to show how *The Beggar's Opera* marks a step from comedy toward an equally worthy genre: tragi-comedy.

3. TRAGEDY AND COMEDY: GENERALISATIONS

We conventionally consider comedy a gay and lighthearted form of art, and we regard any contrasting element as secondary, an undertone, an interruption, an exception. I am proposing, instead, to regard misery as the basis of comedy, and gaiety as an ever-recurring transcendence. Seen in this way, comedy, like tragedy, is a way of trying to cope with despair, mental suffering, guilt and anxiety. But not the same way. The tragic injunction, in the words of Stein, in *Lord Jim*, is: 'in the destructive element, immerse!' It is: walk, like Rilke, with death inside you! Take terror by the hand! More prosaically put: accept the obstacles life places in your way, and confront them! Now, of course, the comic stance is comparatively opportunistic. Its strategy is to evade and elude the enemy, rather than to tackle him. Inevitably the moralists will say that, where tragedy is heroic and sublime, comedy is cowardly and frivolous – like Falstaff, its banner carrier. Serving survival better than morals, and traditionally hostile to the professional moralists, it will get better marks in biology than in religion. But since the goods it advertises are definitely pleasures, though it may lack champions, it can never lack customers.

The pleasures it peddles are, in the first instance, those of farce; for the higher forms include the lower. But, just as the satisfactions of tragedy transcend those of melodrama, so those of comedy transcend those of farce. . . . In tragedy, fear turns to awe. And awe, whatever its intellectual content, if any, is an affirmative feeling, an inspired and numinous feeling, bordering upon ecstasy. The intensity and beauty of awe are in direct ratio to the quantity of horror overcome. Now it is much the same with that higher pleasure of comedy which we call joy. We can receive it only from an author in whom we sense joy's opposite. The comic dramatist's starting point is misery; the joy at his destination is a superb and thrilling transcendence. Given the misery of the human condition in general, what could be more welcome?

Tragedy is one long lament. Not restrained or elegaic but plangent and full-throated, it speaks all the pity of life and the terror. The comic poet does not speak his feelings directly but veils them, contradicts them with pranks or elegancies. It is not necessarily the feelings themselves that differ from those of tragedy; it can rather be the way they are veiled. Comedy is indirect, ironical. It says fun when it means misery. And when it lets the misery show, it is able to transcend it in joy.

All kinds of things have been said about the ending of *The Misanthrope*, but no one that I heard of ever suggested that Alceste will kill himself. He might be a more consistent character if he did. But it is tragic characters who are consistent in that way. 'We are people', says Jean Anouilh's Antigone, 'who ask questions right up to the end.' That is just what Sophocles's Oedipus does despite Jocasta's warnings. In tragedy, but by no means in comedy, the self-preservation instinct is overruled.

At the core of any good tragedy is a profound disturbance of the human equilibrium. This is transcended, at least aesthetically, in the poem itself; and such aesthetic transcendence argues a kind of courage. It is not so clear that each comedy reflects a particular experience of this kind. One cannot tell, because even if the experience were there, comedy would shield it from sight. What one can tell is that the comic writer knows about such things in his bones.

The tragic poet writes from a sense of crisis. It would never be hard to believe of any tragedy that it sprang from a particular crisis in the life of its author. The comic poet is less apt to write out of a particular crisis than from that steady ache of misery which in human life is even more common than crisis and so a more insistent problem. When we get up tomorrow morning, we may well be able to do without our tragic awareness for an hour or two, but we shall desperately need our sense of the comic.

Tragedy says, with the Book of Common Prayer: 'In the midst of life we are in death.' The paradox of this sentiment is that, as it sinks in, the sense of life, of living, is renewed. And the man who truly feels that 'the readiness is all' attains a rare serenity, not only in dying but in living. Comedy says, 'In the midst of death we are in life.' Whatever the hazards of air travel, we continue to plan for the morrow. We are not often in the mood of the tragic hero just before his end, when he has attained to a complete stillness of the will. 'The readiness is all' is a noble sentiment but the exact reverse of it also has its human point. 'I warmed both hands before the fire of life' (so William Lyon Phelps parodied Landor); 'It fades and I'm not ready to depart.'

The desire to live is not merely love of living. It is also greed. Comedy deals with the itch to own the material world. Hence its interest in gluttons who imbibe part of this world, and misers who hoard another part. And from *devouring* and *clutching*, human nature makes a swift leap to *grabbing*. In how many comic plots there is theft or the intention of theft! If men did not wish to break the tenth commandment, comic plotting, as we know it, could never have come into being.

It is possible that in my discussion [in an earlier chapter – Ed.] ... I gave tragedy too benign an image. This would be the time to add that very often the subject of tragedy is not dying but killing. Tragic stories from *Agamemnon* to *Macbeth*, and from *The Duchess of Malfi* to *Penthesilia*, embody the impulse to kill. People who express surprise at the piles of corpses on the tragic stage are asking tragedy to reflect their actions, and they have not committed murder; but tragedy reflects their souls, and in their souls they *have* committed murder. Modern psychology, with its intensive study of daily living, daily imagining, has had no trouble demonstrating the ubiquity of murderous wishes. A human being, in sober fact, needs very little provocation to wish his neighbor dead. The joke behind the joke in the colloquial use of 'Drop dead!' is that the phrase means exactly what it says. Children of three are also taken to be joking when they tell a parent they wish he or she were dead. The joke is on the parent, and it is gallows-humor at that.

Comedy is very often about theft, exactly as tragedy is very often about murder. Just as the tragic poets present few scenes of dying or being dead but many (on stage or off) of killing, so comedy has fewer scenes of possession than of expropriation (or the plan to expropriate). There is a technical reason in both cases: it is of the nature of dramatic art to show, not states of being, but what people do to people. Death is a state, possession is a state, murder and theft are what people do to people. But there is a non-technical reason for the technical reason – as in art there always is. Drama, the art of the extreme, seeks out the ultimate act that corresponds to ultimate fact. In the tragic world, if death is the ultimate fact, the infliction of death is the ultimate act. In the comic world, if possession is the ultimate fact, dispossession is the ultimate act. The motor forces are hatred and greed respectively.

To steal is to falsify, for it is to forge, as it were, a title to ownership. The greed we find in comedy is an offshoot of the spirit of falsehood and mendacity. St John's gospel speaks of Satan as both 'the father of lies' and 'a murderer from the beginning', and this is to say that the mischief in both comedy and tragedy is the very Devil and, conversely, that Satan has a great traditional genre to report each of his two favorite pastimes. 'And of these two diabolical manifestations', a recent theological commentator adds, 'it is arguable that falsity is the more essentially Satanic.' It is arguable, as we have seen, that comedy is a blacker art than tragedy.

The other face of the greed in comedy is tenacity, by which men survive. It is hard to survive. The tragic hero, at the last, can attain to the readiness and ripeness that are all. The rest of us, first and last, cling to existence and on our deathbeds will regret only, as Fontenelle did on his in 1757, that it is so 'difficult to be'. '*Je sens une difficulté d'être*', he said, 'I am finding it difficult to be.' It is a difficulty, like death itself, that permeates all of life. As Jean Cocteau puts it:

In the last analysis, everything can be taken care of except the difficulty of being: the difficulty of being cannot be taken care of.

In the last analysis, it cannot. This comedy knows, and acknowledges in sadness or cynicism. And yet we do not live only in the last analysis, but serially, in analyses first, second, and third. Though in the last analysis, no priest and no physician can stop us from dying, it may be a comfort to have both of them on call until finally we are dead. The comic sense tries to cope with the daily, hourly, inescapable difficulty of being. For if everyday life has an undercurrent or cross-current of the tragic, the main current is material for comedy.

Yet, if comedy begins in the kitchen and the bedroom, it can walk out under the stars. It can attain to grandeur. If this is not generally admitted, it is only because any comedy that has grandeur is immediately stamped as Not a Comedy. (Someone should make an anthology of the various great works that have been called Not a Comedy, Not a Tragedy, and Not a Play. It would be one of the Hundred Great Books.) A comedy that achieves grandeur is also said to be veering toward tragedy. There is seldom any plausibility to the attribution. If any of these comedies were subtitled A Tragedy it would be said to be toppling toward Comedy.

Molière's *Don Juan* is an example. There is something marvellously lofty and mysterious about it. One would be at a loss to name any tragedy with an atmosphere of this type. The weighty world of tragedy is created the direct way: with weighty words to which in the theatre is added weighty acting. The world of Molière's *Don Juan* is created by the traditional dialectic of farce and comedy, that is, indirectly, with the weight only suggested, what is actually said and acted kept studiously flippant.

To think of Molière's *Don Juan* is to think of Mozart's *Don Giovanni*. Mozart also used the comic dialectic: it exactly corresponded to his own mentality, as it had to Molière's. Mozart early attached himself to the tradition of great comic theatre: he had completed a setting of a Goldoni play at the age of twelve. *La finta semplice* is musical farce. His development from there to *Così fan tutte* and *Don Giovanni* is not a progress toward tragedy. It is a progress from farce to comedy. What grows is his power to suggest the immensity of what lies underneath. But the comic surface is resolutely and scintillatingly maintained. To call *Don Giovanni* tragic makes no sense. We are in no way encouraged to identify ourselves with the Don's guilt. So far is such an attitude from Mozart that he can show the death of the Don (as Jonson shows us Volpone punished) without winning sympathy for him. The work is called tragic only by those who refuse to consider the possibility that such immensity and terror might be within the scope of comedy.

Though there are so many differences between tragedy and comedy, it is news as old as Plato that the two have something in common. Scholars are not agreed as to how to take the passage in the *Symposium* in which this point is made but, thinking for ourselves, and with so much drama to think about which Plato did not know, we can see that the two genres stand together in very many ways. For example, they stand in contrast to an art such as music which glories in the direct expression of affirmative sentiments like the feeling of triumph. Tragedy and comedy are alike negative arts in that they characteristically reach positive statements by inference from negative situations. 'In stories like this', says the Gardener in Giraudoux's *Electra*, 'the people won't stop killing and biting each other to tell you the one aim of life is love.'

Surprising though it may be, the ego takes as much punishment in comedy as in tragedy, even if it is the pretensions of knaves and fools that are cut down, and not the rashness of a hero. Both tragedy and comedy demonstrate, with plots and characters that provide horribly conclusive evidence, that life is not worth living; and yet they finally convey such a sense of the majesty of our sufferings or the poignancy of our follies that, lo and behold! – the enterprise seems worth having been a part of. Both tragedy and comedy are about human weakness, but both, in the end, testify to human strength. In tragedy one is glad to be identified with a hero, whatever his flaw or his fate. In comedy, even if one cannot identify oneself with anybody on stage, one has a hero to identify with, nonetheless: the author. One is proud to be lent the spectacles of Jonson or Molière.

Like tragedy, comedy can achieve a transcendence over misery, an aesthetic transcendence (of art over life), and a transcending emotion (awe in tragedy, joy in comedy). Both tragedy and comedy amount to an affirmation made irrationally – that is, in defiance of the stated facts – like religious affirmation. Unlike the church, however, the theatre claims no metaphysical status for such affirmations.

Finally, tragedy and comedy have the same heuristic intent: self-knowledge. What tragedy achieves in this line by its incredibly direct rendering of sympathies and antipathies, comedy achieves by indirection, duality, irony. As Northrop Frye says, comedy is 'designed, not to condemn evil, but to ridicule a lack of self-knowledge'. [See essay included in this selection – Ed.] To condemn evil would be direct, single, unironic, and therefore uncomic. To spend one's life condemning evil has all too often been to lack self-knowledge and to fail to see this. The classic condemners of evil are the Pharisees. And the Pharisees, then and now, cannot make use of comedy; they can only be made use of by it.

Molière, says Fernandez, 'teaches us the unspeakably difficult art of seeing ourselves in spite of ourselves'. We are mistaken about our own identities: comedy makes of mistaken identity a classic subject. And if 'to be mistaken about' is a passive phenomenon, it has its active counterpart. We are not only mistaken in ourselves but the cause that mistakes are in other men. Deceiving ourselves, we deceive our fellows. Now the art of comedy is an undeceiving, an emancipation from error, an unmasking, an art, if you will, of dénouement or 'untying'. But a knot cannot be untied without first having been tied. A dénouement comes at the end: through most of the play we have in fact been fooled. Thus, by a truly comic paradox, the playwright who exposes our trickery does so by out-tricking us. In that respect, he is his own chief knave, and has made of us, his audience, his principal fool. The bag of tricks of this prince of knaves is – the art of comedy.

4.   AS YOU LIKE IT

I hope the foregoing generalisations are clear, but, if they are, they must also be too simple, too definite and too schematic to correspond to all the facts. Categories, as Bernard Berenson put it, are only a compromise with chaos. And having used them, we do well to renew contact with the chaos and ask what damage a particular compromise has done.

The history of the arts is full of discrepancies between theory and practice, nomenclature and fact. For example, the word comedy is generally used – and not only by the amateur – in a sense too narrow to cover all comedies. In his essay on laughter, Henri Bergson's performance is one to hold any intelligent reader spellbound; but when one puts down the book one realises that this dazzling piece of theory leaves no room in comic writing for Shakespeare. [See excerpt in Part Two, above – Ed.]

And this is due to no peculiar limitation of the great French philosopher. It is due to the fact that the way we all discuss comedy grows out of one tradition of comedy and covers the case of that tradition alone. Since this is the classical or Latin tradition, coming down from Greek New Comedy through Plautus and Terence to Machiavelli and Ben Jonson and Molière, it has some application to comic writers of all schools. Even Shakespeare made an adaptation from Plautus. Yet by this time perhaps anyone but a Frenchman would admit that a kind of comedy has come into being that differs almost as much from Latin comedy as either kind of comedy differs from tragedy. *A Midsummer Night's Dream*, for example, differs from *The Alchemist* as much as either differs from *Hamlet*.

Writing of each genre *en bloc*, as I am, I would have been content to go on writing of comedy *en bloc*, except for the excessive degree of distortion entailed. It is not that a conventional list of types (comedy of manners, of humours, of character) is needed to illuminate the life of comedy, but that to speak of Shakespeare and Molière, Jonson and Mozart, in one breath, as I have just done, leaves an impression of a single tradition and a single method. All minor categories and subtler distinctions aside, it seems to me that the history of comedy bears witness to two traditions, two methods of quite contrary tendency.

A hint of the divergence has already been provided in my discussion of jokes. Following Freud, I distinguished two kinds of jokes, the harmless and the purposive. Only the purposive or tendentious joke, it was remarked, had enough violence in it to be useful in farce. This kind of joke is at the root, not only of farce, but of comedy in the Latin tradition. The harmless joke is rooted in sympathy, the purposive joke in scorn. The main or Latin tradition of comedy is scornful comedy. Its weapon is ridicule. But sympathy, if not of much use in farce, can be abundantly used in comedy. When it is at the heart of comedy, we have comedy of a radically un-Latin sort – such as Shakespeare's or Mozart's.

This idea can be elaborated by recourse to the old distinction between wit and humor. Making use of this distinction we must probably define all comedy before the Elizabethans, and most French comedy afterwards, as comedy of wit. (Nervous about the word *humeur*, the French resort to the English word *humour* to describe that evidently un-French thing.) The tradition of humor is the tradition of Shakespeare and Cervantes, Sterne and Jean-Paul Richter, Dickens and Charlie Chaplin, Manzoni and Pirandello, Gogol and Chekhov and Sholem Aleichem.

Pirandello clarifies the old distinction in his essay, 'L'umore', when he remarks that if you see an old woman with dyed hair and too much make-up, and she strikes you as ridiculous, you have only to go on thinking about her to find her sad. 'Humor' in writing is to include both these elements, where 'wit' would rest content with the first. Wit and humor are therefore not simple opposites, since humor includes wit. Still, a comedy that is rooted in humor may well emerge so different from a comedy rooted in wit that generalisation about comedy will not be equally true of both.

For example, my own definition of comic dialectic. The main dynamic contrast, as I have presented it, is between a frivolous manner and a grim meaning. The tone says: life is fun. The undertone suggests that life is a catastrophe. The extreme instance is the kind of comedy in which the final curtain has to fall to save us from a veritable cataclysm.

Now though this formula may apply to particular scenes in Shakespearean comedy, and to early plays like *A Comedy of Errors* and *The Taming of the Shrew*, it does not cover any of his mature comedies as a whole. In *Twelfth Night*, for instance, the brio of Latin comedy is not in evidence during most of the play. The tone of most of the scenes is not flippant or frivolous or skittish or clever or elegant. The atmosphere is not even, in the everyday sense, 'comic'. It is that of 'romance' in the old sense – a tale of wonder and misadventure. The misadventures are on the grand scale, the scale of the 'terrible'. Yet – and this is the contrast on which the play is based – a happy ending is somehow implicit from the beginning. A very curious blend: something close to tragedy is counteracted by a kind of magic or hocus-pocus of comedy-with-a-happy-ending. A surface of the 'terrible' conceals beneath it a kind of cosmic beneficence, a metaphysically guaranteed good luck. Such is the 'contrary tendency' in our second tradition of comedy, which reveals itself as a kind of inversion of the first: for grim statements in a gay style are substituted benign statements in a style not without solemnity.

The two kinds of comedy would seem to have different ends in view. In the logic of the first is a shock effect in the shape of a revelation of what is horrible. This kind of play seems to drive inward toward the forbidding truth. Its 'happy ending' is purely ironical. In the logic of the second kind of comedy is an effect of enchantment in the shape of an apparent realisation of our fondest hopes – that is, our hopes for love and happiness. Its happy ending is not only not ironical; it is, in effect, spread through the play; when it finally supervenes, it is a fitting culmination. 'I was only joking' and 'Let's not go into that' give place to 'As you like it'.

What does such an ending mean? Does it offer comforting truth to offset the grimmer truth of witty comedy? Comfortable, philistine critics will wish to think so. It is the tendency of this 'romantic' comedy to create a 'romantic' atmosphere in which the possibility of happiness and love arises – but whether as illusion or reality remains forever uncertain. The signature of this kind of comedy is a loveliness which can be 'reality itself' or the 'veil of illusion' – as you will. Here the Shakespearean 'what you will' touches the Pirandellian 'as you wish me' and 'it is so if it seems to you'. Love dissolves in the cosmic mystery of illusion and reality.

> A great while ago the world begun
> With a hey ho, the wind and the rain,
> But that's all one, our play is done,
> And we'll strive to please you every day.

We'll strive to please you. Our play will be exactly as you like it. As for its meaning (illusion? reality?), we have pleased you, and you shall please yourselves. The world of our play shall be as you like it; also the world outside our play.... Thus, with a pun on the verb *to like*, is 'solved' the ultimate problem of metaphysics.

Mozart often worked from plays and libretti in the Latin tradition, but his own contribution was of the Shakespearean sort. Beaumarchais' *Marriage of Figaro* ends with the kind of improbability which we are to recognise as such and take ironically. 'In real life', we are to go home saying, 'things couldn't be patched up this way: Almaviva was a wolf and would continue so'. In the Mozart opera, the patching-up is preceded by a different work, different, most of all, in that the 'romantic' feelings of the characters have been made fully real to the audience, as in a Shakespeare comedy. Thus it is that the lovely notes Mozart has set to the Count's request to be forgiven, and to the Countess's accession to the request, can come as a true, unironical climax. Life is seen here, not through the eyes of the worldly, witty, Gallic Beaumarchais, but through those of a spiritual and humorous Austrian. In Mozart's *Marriage of Figaro*, as in *Twelfth Night*, love and happiness have their reality in art, while the question of their reality in life is left in uncynical abeyance.

Two kinds of comedy, one that moves toward unresolved discord, one that moves just as irresistibly toward complete concord: give to either of these a little more tragic an emphasis, and we shall get tragi-comedy. Suppose, for instance, after the discord of the first kind of comedy, more scenes were added, and the earlier scenes were then adjusted to these extra ones. A play like *Celestina* would result. Or suppose the kind of comedy that ends in true concord were proceeded by misadventures of a more malignant sort, as in *The Winter's Tale*.

SOURCE: ch. 9 on 'Comedy' in *The Life of the Drama* (New York, 1964; London, 1965), pp. 295–315).

Elder Olson   'The Comic Object'
(1968)

... Properly speaking ... the comic includes only the ridiculous, the ludicrous, the things which are taken as such by analogy, the witty and the humorous. All of these, differ as they may, have a common characteristic: their minimisation of the claim of some particular thing to be taken seriously, either by reducing that claim to absurdity, or by reducing it merely to the negligible in such a way as to produce pleasure by that very minimisation. The comic object must, first of all, then, be something which may be thought to present such a claim: for what does not exist cannot be minimised. Thus, something that we already regard as of no value whatsoever, either in itself or in relation to anything else, is not a comic object; it is rather an object of indifference. The comic object must either excite some degree of desire or aversion, or afford the basis *for the inception* of some emotion, or promote the anticipation of one of these; it may simply evoke curiosity or wonder, which involve a desire to know, or it may present us with something apparently fearful or pathetic. On the other hand, it must not arouse desire or aversion or emotion to such a degree that they cannot easily be extinguished. For it is precisely by the destruction or annihilation of the *ground* of the desire or aversion or emotion that the comic operates. ...

THE RELAXATION OF CONCERN

In investigating the nature of the comic [in Olson's previous discussion – Ed.], we found that it was not so much a question of laughter as of the restoration of the mind to a certain condition. This, we said, was a pleasant, or rather a euphoric, condition of freedom from desires and emotions which move men to action, and one in which we were inclined to take nothing seriously and to be gay about everything. The *transition* to this state was effected through a special kind of relaxation of concern: a *katastasis*, as I called it, of concern through the annihilation of the concern itself – not by the substitution for desire of its contrary, aversion, nor by the replacement, say, of fear, by the contrary emotion of hope, which is also serious, but by the conversion of the *grounds* of concern into absolutely nothing. I gave you as an example a common form of joke which presents something as remarkable, only to disclose that it was something either perfectly ordinary or else impossible; so that it removed our concern – in this case our curiosity – not by gratifying it but by destroying the curiosity itself. This was produced either by the ridiculous or the ludicrous themselves, or by the wit or humor which exposed them to us as such; and I went on to show what things we take seriously, and in what respects the ridiculous and the ludicrous are their contraries. I said a good deal more, and shall have a good deal more to say about these matters; for the moment this will suffice.

Our present problem is the nature of comedy; and many critics have insisted that we must distinguish between the comic and comedy itself. They are quite right: the comic is a certain quality, and comedy, as I am taking it, is a certain form of drama. The former may apply to things outside art; the latter, to art alone. . . .

THE COMIC VIEW

. . . We may take a grave or a lighthearted view of human life and actions; tragedy develops out of the grave view as comedy does out of the lighthearted. If we take the grave view, life is full of perils and misfortunes which evoke in us fear and pity; if we take the lighthearted view, there is nothing to be greatly concerned about. It is not the events by themselves which are matter for gravity or levity; it is the view taken of them. *Convention* may determine that this is a solemn matter, and not to be joked about; but so far as things themselves are concerned, death, murder, rape, incest are no less matter for comedy than for tragedy. The Oedipus legend served Sophocles as a tragic subject; it would be quite as possible to make it into comedy. When we say, thus, that tragedy imitates a serious action, we mean that it imitates an action *which it makes serious*; and comparably, comedy imitates an action *which it makes a matter for levity*.

If it is now clear what imitation is and what catharsis is, it should be clear what comedy is and what it effects. It has no catharsis, since all the kinds of the comic – the ridiculous and ludicrous, for example – are naturally pleasant. Tragedy exhausts pity and fear by arousing these emotions to their utmost and by providing them with their most perfect objects; it excites concern and directs it into its proper channel; it brings the mind into its normal condition by energising its capacity for painful emotion. Comedy, on the other hand, removes concern by showing that it was absurd to think that there was ground for it. Tragedy endows with worth; comedy takes the worth away. Tragedy exhibits life as directed to important ends; comedy as either not directed to such ends, or unlikely to achieve them.

If we call action of the latter sort *valueless*, we may define comedy as an imitation of valueless action, in language, performed and not narrated, effecting a katastasis of concern through the absurd. To this definition we must add such qualifications of magnitude, completeness, etc., as Aristotle does; but the main points are, I hope, clear.

On this account of the whole, it is clear that comedy must consist of the same number of parts as tragedy – that is, the six parts of plot, character, thought, diction, music, and spectacle – but that these parts cannot be of the same quality as those of tragedy, for in that case tragedy and comedy would be identical.

We must discuss this point later; for the moment, let us consider the comic action and the kind of personage we properly call comic. I have just called the comic action 'worthless' or 'valueless'. This is a translation of the Greek *phaulos*. I may explain this, perhaps, by contrasting it with the tragic action. The tragic action produces pity and fear – 'pity', says Aristotle, 'for the man suffering undeserved misfortune; fear for the man like ourselves'. The comic action is the precise opposite of this: the comic character, as I argued earlier, is *unlike us, in so far as he is comic*, and the misfortunes, in so far as they are comic, either are not grave or are deserved. The comic action, thus, neutralises the emotions of pity and fear to produce the *contrary* – again

I must insist, not the negative or contradictory but *the contrary* – of the serious.

We must also observe that not every serious action is tragic, and that, comparably, not every 'worthless' action is comic; a tragic action is a serious action which has been constructed so as to have the power or *dynamis* of producing pity and fear, and the comic action is the worthless action which has been so constructed as to have the power of the emotion conducive to laughter. Moreover, not even every serious action which arouses pity and fear is tragic; but only that kind which catharts these emotions; and similarly, not every worthless action, even when involving laughter, is comic, but only the kind which effects *katastasis* or relaxation, i.e., by affording the perfect object for this emotion.

The question may arise of what we may mean by 'the proper object of emotion'; for obviously people pity or fear different things, and some take seriously what others do not. The multiplicity and diversity of reaction has often been cited as an impassable obstacle to any general theory. Perhaps it is not impassable after all. Surely here as elsewhere we must take the sound as a standard by which we judge the unsound, and not mingle all together as if they had an equal claim to consideration; it would be foolish, for instance, to accept the word of a man with poor vision as equally authoritative with that of the man whose vision is excellent. Here, similarly, we must take the word of the brave man rather than that of a coward as to what is really fearful, and thus generally the word of the virtuous person; so that what is really pitiful or fearful, or serious or comic, is what is so in the judgement of the man of practical wisdom. Hence, while anything may be ridiculed, it is only the really ridiculous which is *properly* ridiculed; and it is only proper ridicule that really produces the comic response, for it alone produces pleasure through the ridiculous as such. Otherwise ridicule either stems from what is unpleasant or produces displeasure; for example, a great many jokes are really kinds of aggression; those who laugh at them laugh because they feel hatred for the object ridiculed, and hatred is always of something painful; and other people are offended by jokes of this order. Those who take pleasure in jokes or ridicule of this kind are pleased because it is pleasant to think that the object of their hatred is utterly valueless, though the fact that they hate it shows that they are pained by it and therefore do attribute to it a value which they are unwilling to admit.

From these observations it is evident that as imitations tragedy and comedy offer us likenesses of the tragic and ridiculous which we recognise as such, and in their universal aspect, although manifested through particulars; and that it is upon such recognition that our emotional responses are contingent. Thus imitation affords the pleasure both of learning – through recognising the ridiculous thing precisely as ridiculous, for example – and of emotional satisfaction; though the latter is clearly contingent upon the former. In their proper nature, therefore, the arts offer us proper moral perceptions. They cannot in so doing make us virtuous, for virtue is a habit which can only be produced by action; they can supply us with knowledge of what is good or bad, whether we act on it or not; and they do this not for the sake of such knowledge but in fulfillment of their own nature. From this their ethical and political value is easily apparent, as well as why they are helpful to good societies and governments and dangerous to the bad.

To put this a little differently: comedy and tragedy differ basically in the value which they induce us to set upon the actions which they depict; and one and the same act, seen in contrary lights, produces contrary effects. This is surely what Shaw had in mind in the Preface to *Saint Joan* when, speaking of her burning, he remarks: 'At such murders the angels weep; but the gods laugh at the murderers.' The angels see the action in terms of the undeserved anguish and death of the victim; the gods see it in terms of the folly which motivates it and which makes it absurdly incapable of achieving its proposed end. In their less than divine wisdom the angels respond with more than human pity; the wiser gods see only the folly of man. . . .

THE STANDARDS THAT DETERMINE ABSURDITY

. . . What the comic is in general I expounded in the preceding chapters. I defined it as something that produced a relaxation of concern by exhibiting an apparent absurdity in the grounds of concern, and I stated that the comic response depended on three conditions: to state it in terms of laughter (though you remember it was not necessarily a matter of laughter), (1) the kind of person laughed at, (2) the frame of mind of the laugher, and (3) the particular cause of the laughter – all of which I analysed at length. The problem, I think, is insoluble except in terms of these conditions, for otherwise, as I showed, we get into the endless business of asking about what a Hottentot or an Eskimo laughs at, and so on. Now it involves the absurd, and, as I argued, the absurd is seen only by comparison with a standard. And standards vary, for they are opinions of what is right and proper in any given instance, and such opinions vary with the class and education, intelligence and character and so on, of the people who hold them. Again, a judgement is reached by means of the standard, i.e., a judgement that the thing is absurd, and such judgements may be right or wrong: something may be judged as absurd when it is not. And there are different standards, too, of what should or should not be laughed at, for brutal persons may laugh at a man who is being led to execution, or at the commission of some great crime. Of course we judge these standards themselves; and so we get such classifications of humor as gross or refined, brutal or humane, intelligent or stupid or silly, or the like. Thus this joke is revolting, while that one is stupid, and another is clever; and we are talking about comic quality. These are clearly moral distinctions; they are very relevant indeed; but they cannot be made by artistic principles, for they belong to ethics; art rather assumes them, bases on them, does not establish them.

Source: extracts from *The Theory of Comedy* (Bloomington, Indiana, 1968), pp. 23, 25–6, 35–9, 61–2.

SELECT BIBLIOGRAPHY

Students are advised to consult the complete books from which extracts have been reprinted in this selection. The following additional studies are also recommended.

Erich Auerbach, *Mimesis: The Representation of Reality in Western Literature*, trans. Willard Trask (Princeton, N. J., 1953; paperback edn, New York, 1957).

C. L. Barber, *Shakespeare's Festive Comedy* (Princeton, N. J., 1959).

Albert Cook, *The Dark Voyage and the Golden Mean: A Philosophy of Comedy* (Cambridge, Mass., 1949).

Lane Cooper, *An Aristotelian Theory of Comedy* (New York, 1922).

Robert W. Corrigan (ed.), *Comedy: Meaning and Form* (Scranton, Penn., 1965).

Sigmund Freud, *Jokes and Their Relation to the Unconscious*, trans. James Strachey (London, 1960: new edn New York, 1963; London, 1966).

Martin Grotjahn, *Beyond Laughter: Humor and the Subconscious* (New York, 1957).

Morton Gurewitch, *The Irrational Vision* (Ithaca, N.Y., 1975).

Arthur Koestler, *The Act of Creation* (London, 1969).

L. J. Potts, *Comedy* (London, 1948).

Fred Miller Robinson, *The Comedy of Language* (Amherst, Mass., 1980).

Leo Salingar, *Shakespeare and the Traditions of Comedy* (Cambridge, 1974).

Bernard Schilling, *The Comic Spirit* (Detroit, 1967).

Wylie Sypher (ed.), *Comedy* (New York, 1956).

Enid Welsford, *The Fool* (London, 1935).

NOTES ON CONTRIBUTORS

ARISTOTLE (384–322 BC): Greek philosopher; in *Poetics* he sought to describe the form and function of tragedy and epic – and possibly, in a lost part, of comedy; the work was intended to counter the views of Socrates and Plato about the role and craft of the artist.

MIKHAIL BAKHTIN: leader of a Russian school of structuralist criticism since the 1930s. His first book, *Problems of Dostoevesky's Poetics* (1929; trans. R.W. Rostel, 1973) interprets the language in the Russian novelist's fiction as an interplay of voices encoding the relationship between speakers and listeners, author and characters. His study of Rabelais (excerpted in this selection) was written in 1940, but not published until 1965; it extends the conception of semiotic systems in literature from verbal language to forms of cultural expression (in this case, of laughter) such as folk rites and festivities.

ERIC BENTLEY: British-born American dramatic critic, translator and playwright; Katharine Cornell Professor of Drama, State University of New York since 1975, having previously taught dramatic literature at Columbia University.

HENRI LOUIS BERGSON (1859–1941): Fench philosopher, exponent of the *élan vital* (life force) theory and supporter of creative against analytic thinking, notably in *Matière et Mémoire* (1896) and *L'Evolution créatrice* (1907); Nobel prize-winner for Literature, 1927.

MARCUS TULLIUS CICERO (106–43 BC): Roman orator, writer and statesman; his treatises on rhetoric and philosophical questions were greatly influenced by Greek writers and thinkers.

WILLIAM CONGREVE (1670–1729): playwright and critic of the drama; his comedies are among the greatest works of the genre in English.

FRANCIS M. CORNFORD (1874–1943): Classical scholar at Cambridge and Professor of Ancient Philosophy (1931–9) in that university; author of several works, including *The Origin of Attic Comedy*, and known to a wider public for his *Microcosmographia Academica* (1908), a skit on academic politics which still gives refreshment to undergraduates and dons in the English-speaking world.

R. S. CRANE (1886–1967): for many years Professor of English, University of Chicago, and editor of the *Philological Quarterly*; his publications include *The Languages of Criticism and the Structure of Poetry* (1953) and *The Idea of the Humanities and Other Essays Critical and Historical*, 2 vols (1967).

DANTE ALIGHIERI (1265-1321): Italian poet and writer on politics; pre-eminent in poetic inspiration and technique, his major works are *La Vita Nuova* and *The Divine Comedy*, of which there are many English versions, old and new.

IAN DONALDSON: Professor of English, Australian National University, and a former co-editor of *Essays in Criticism*; his publications include *The World Upside-Down: Comedy from Jonson to Fielding* (1970) and the Oxford edition of Jonson's *Poems* (1975).

FRIEDRICH DÜRRENMATT: Swiss dramatist and novelist; his plays – notably *The Old Lady's Visit* (1956) and *The Physicists* (1962) – are often experimental in form and satirically mocking of conventional values he regards as hypocritical.

EVANTHIUS (4th century AD): a grammarian whose treatise on comedy, itself based on Alexandrian accounts of the drama, was incorporated in an essay, 'De tragoedia et comoedia', attributed to his contemporary, Aelius Donatus. Since Donatus was the author of a commentary on the comedies of Terence, the essay was often printed in Renaissance editions of the Roman playwright and thereby became an important means of transmitting late-classical ideas of comedy to Renaissance scholars and dramatists.

HENRY FIELDING (1707-54): novelist, dramatist and Bow Street magistrate; his fiction includes *Joseph Andrews* (1742), *Jonathan Wild* (1743), *Tom Jones* (1749) and (it is believed) *Shamela* (1741), a parody of Richardson's *Pamela*.

NORTHROP FRYE: Canadian literary critic, since 1967 University Professor of English, Massey College, University of Toronto; his many publications, which have had a wide influence, include *Anatomy of Criticism: Four Essays* (1957, and new editions), *Fables of Identity: Studies in Poetic Mythology* (1963), *The Well-Tempered Critic* (1963), *A Natural Perspective: The Development of Shakespearean Comedy and Romance* (1965), *On Teaching Literature* (1972), *The Secular Scripture: A Study of the Structure of Romance* (1976) and *Spiritus Mundi: Essays on Literature, Myth and Society* (1977).

OLIVER GOLDSMITH (1730-74): Anglo-Irish poet, novelist, playwright and essayist; his critical writings include, in addition to his essays on the theatre, *An Enquiry into the Present State of Polite Learning* (1759).

WILLIAM HAZLITT (1778-1830): essayist, literary critic and political writer; his dramatic criticism for London journals was assembled in *A View of the English Stage* (1818); his essays on literary criticism – notably *Characters of Shakespeare's Plays* (1817-18), *Lectures on the English Poets* (1818-19) and *English Comic Writers* (1819) – are important expressions of 'Romantic' sensibility and of the popularisation of literary criticism in serious form.

BEN JONSON (1572-1637): dramatist and poet; besides his own works – including two supreme comedies: *Volpone* and *The Alchemist* – he was influential as a critic and as a counsellor to younger writers.

WALTER KAISER: Professor of Comparative Literature, Harvard University; in addition to *Praisers of Folly*, his publications include an edition (1964) of John Florio's *The Essays of Montaigne* (first published 1603), and his translation (1969) of *Three Secret Poems* by the modern Greek poet, George Seferis.

CHARLES LAMB (1775–1834): essayist and critic; his discernment did much to advance appreciation of Shakespeare and to revive interest in the older school of English dramatists; he is today best known for his *Essays of Elia* (1820–23).

SUSANNE LANGER: formerly Professor of Philosophy, Connecticut College; her other works on aesthetics include *Philosophy in a New Key* (1942) and *Philosophical Sketches* (1962).

GEORGE MEREDITH (1828–1900): poet, novelist and critic; of his novels *The Egoist* (1879) and *Diana of the Crossways* (1885) have been most esteemed by literary critics, though *The Ordeal of Richard Feverel* (1859), *Harry Richmond* (1870–71) and *Beauchamp's Career* (1875–76) have been less esoteric to the general reader; *Modern Love* (1862) is now regarded as one of the outstanding poetical works of the nineteenth century.

ELDER OLSON: American poet, playwright and literary critic; Professor of English, University of Chicago since 1954; his critical studies include *Critics and Criticism*, with others (1952), *Tragedy and the Theory of Drama* (1961), *The Theory of Comedy* (1968) and *On Value Judgements in the Arts, and Other Essays* (1976); his poetry has been published in *Collected Poems* (1963) and in *Olson's Penny Arcade* (1975).

PLATO (429–347 BC): Greek philosopher, pupil and interpreter of Socrates; in both the *Republic* and his other writings, Plato's views on poetry and the arts, on the nature and the role of the imagination, had – and continue to exert – an enormous influence, despite challenging criticism and modifications of them from Aristotle to the present day.

SIR PHILIP SIDNEY (1554–86): poet, courtier, man of letters and soldier, perhaps the most noted English type of the 'complete gentleman' of Renaissance idealisation; his *An Apologie for Poetrie* (1580, published 1595) – alternatively styled *Defence of Poesie* – is a landmark in the development of English literary criticism.

NICHOLAS UDALL (1505–56): dramatist and scholar; successively headmaster at Eton and Westminster, his *Ralph Roister Doister* (c. 1553) is the first full-length English comedy.

ACKNOWLEDGEMENTS

The editor and publishers wish to thank the following for permission to use copyright material: Mikhail Bakhtin, extract from *Rabelais and His World*, 1968, translated by Helene Iswolsky, by permission of The MIT Press, Cambridge, Massachusetts; Eric Bentley, chapter 'Comedy' from *The Life of the Drama*, 1965, by permission of Laurence Pollinger Ltd on behalf of the author; Cicero, extract from *De Oratore* translated by E. W. Sutton and H. Rackham, 1942, by permission of The Loeb Classical Library; F. M. Cornford, extracts from *The Origin of Attic Comedy*, 1914, by permission of Edward Arnold (Publishers) Ltd; R. S. Crane, section III of essay 'The Concept of Plot and the Plot of *Tom Jones*' in *Critics and Criticism: Ancient and Modern*, 1952, by permission of The University of Chicago Press; Ian Donaldson, extract from *The World Upside-Down: Comedy from Jonson to Fielding*, 1970, by permission of Oxford University Press; Friedrich Dürrenmatt, extract from 'Problems of the Theatre' in *Four Plays, 1957–62*, translated by Gerhard Nellhaus, by permission of Jonathan Cape Ltd; Northrop Frye, essay 'The Argument of Comedy' in *English Institute Essays*, 1948, by permission of Columbia University Press and the author; Walter Kaiser, extract from *Praisers of Folly*, 1964, by permission of Harvard University Press, copyright © 1963 by the President and Fellows of Harvard College; Susanne Langer, extract from *Feeling and Form*, 1953, by permission of Routledge and Kegan Paul Ltd; Elder Olson, extracts from *The Theory of Comedy*, 1968, by permission of Indiana University Press; Plato, extract from *Philebus and Epinomis*, 1956, translated by A. E. Taylor, by permission of Thomas Nelson & Sons Ltd.

INDEX

Page numbers in **bold** type relate to essays or excerpts in this Casebook. Entries in SMALL CAPS denote literary characters.